Fabulous Meals for Busy People

Over 100 Dishes in Under 30 Minutes

by Hannelore Blohm

Woodbury, New York • London • Toronto • Sydney

Hannelore Blohm
Hannelore has been cooking for sheer enjoyment since she was a child. Her career began when she was five — baking cakes, although what this really amounted to was mixing the batter. Her later education prepared her for a career as a newspaper and magazine journalist, and eventually, a professional food writer. She has written several cookbooks, including the *Simple and Quick Diet Cookbook*, published by Barron's.

Credits
Color photographs created by Teubner Studio, Füssen, West Germany, supplemented with pictures from: C.P. Fischer, Baldham (pages 70, 75, 97, 104); Marianne Kaltenbach, Lucerne (55); Lagnese-Iglo GmbH, Hamburg (26, 43, 48, 72, 78, 80, 103); Maggi, Frankfurt (56); and Pfanni, Munich (44).

Original Editor: Nina Andres
Translation: Anne Mendelson
Line Drawings: Ingrid Schütz, Munich

First English language edition published 1986 by Barron's Educational Series, Inc.

Originally published in German under the title
Schnellküche für Berufstätige
©1984 by Grafe und Unzer GmbH, Munich, West Germany

All inquiries should be addressed to:
Barron's Educational Series, Inc.
113 Crossways Park Drive
Woodbury, New York 11797

International Standard Book No. 0-8120-5599-3

Library of Congress Cataloging-in-Publication Data

Blohm, Hannelore.
    Fabulous meals for busy people.

        Translation of: Schnellküche für Berufstätige.
        Includes index.
        1. Cookery. I. Title.
    TX652.B58513 1986 641.5'55 85-26798
    ISBN 0-8120-5599-3

Library of Congress Catalog Card No. 85-26798

PRINTED IN HONG KONG
6 7 8 9   9 8 7 6 5 4 3 2 1

Contents

Preface

Good household organization is critical for anyone with the double responsibility of career and family. With this new time-saving picture cookbook, I'd like to bring practical kitchen advice to all who have such a twofold responsibility—and, above all, to preserve (or restore) for them the pleasure of cooking.

Sound, balanced meals are important for any family, and many people would like to raise their nutritional "awareness quotient." Accordingly, I have sought to make these recipes not only easy to prepare but ample in wholesome and flavorsome nutrition.

The recipe chapters are organized according to preparation time: 15, 20, 25, or at most 30 minutes. The time required for heating electric stove burners has not been included in the time estimates, but preheating times for burners (as well as for electric or gas ovens) can generally fit into the overall preparation schedule, so that they do not significantly affect the total times. In many recipes I have refrained from suggesting a garnish in the interest of saving a few minutes. But with a little parsley, a few tomato slices, quartered hard-cooked eggs, or a couple of radish roses, dishes can be attractively presented in a hurry.

No matter what sort of meal you're planning, your choice will be determined by the time at your disposal. With this book you have the option of choosing, for example, an extra-quick soup or dessert and devoting most of your time to the main dish, or you can pamper your family or guests with a 25-minute dessert if you select a main dish with a substantially shorter preparation time. You'll be confident of delicious recipes, assured of success without stress.

In most cases the menu will include ready-made foods—which, thankfully, are available in ever-greater variety and quality. Nowadays, excellent store-bought salads, pastas, cold meats, cheeses, soups, and so on allow you to plan delicious meals with a minimum of fuss. This book, in addition, will show you how to transform ready-made products into delicious desserts, and which condiments, canned foods, and seasonings you should have in your cupboard in order to be armed against all eventualities.

If the recipe titles don't lend wings to your fancy all by themselves, surely you'll be stimulated by the many color photographs; nearly every recipe is illustrated. I wish you success and hope that with this book you will save a great deal of time and use it profitably.

All recipes have been calculated for 4 servings, unless otherwise noted.

Saving Time in the Kitchen

This book was written especially with two-career couples and working parents in mind. Two-career couples can, ideally, fill in for each other in the kitchen as necessary. The recipes in this book are eminently suited to such arrangements: neither partner needs to be an accomplished cook, and the menus are so quick to prepare that they are very accommodating to the last-minute schedule change or an unexpected delay at the office.

It is probably the working parent who has the least time of all for cooking. The kids are impatient for dinner, and you're looking forward to an evening with the family — or some time to yourself — but not to an hour or two in the kitchen. Take a little time to prepare ahead: if you peel potatoes, trim vegetables, or wash the salad greens in the morning, there will be that less to do at dinnertime. Best of all enlist the children's help with these advance preparations.

Quick but Healthful

Proper nutrition means more than simply eating. How easy it would be if you could just hand a piece of cake (or chocolate or a cookie) to each member of the family for breakfast or lunch! True, they could get filled up on it — but needless to say it would be a terribly unsound regimen.

What you do need to eat are the essential macronutrients (protein, fat, and carbohydrates), metabolic agents (vitamins, minerals, trace elements), and fiber. It is the macronutrients that furnish the body with cellular building blocks, and necessary energy. The metabolic agents must be supplied by the diet because your body can produce hardly any of them by itself. Fiber aids in digestion, among many other functions.

How much nourishment you take in is not an abstract, indifferent question either. As a rough estimate, the energy requirement for adult women lies between 2,000 and 2,200 calories a day; for men, between 2,200 and 2,400 calories. With strenuous physical activity, calorie requirements are of course higher. But in any case, you will lead a healthier life if you are slim. Lean meat, lean fish, lean poultry, low-fat milk products, very little fat, and simple carbohydrates like potatoes, unhulled brown rice, whole-grain pasta, and a lot of fruit and vegetables will help you solve your figure problems. This is the ideal regimen to keep you healthy and fit.

Finally, it is important how you *distribute* the nourishment you take in during the course of the day. Gigantic portions, for instance, make you tired, since an increased amount of blood must be used for the digestive process in the stomach and intestines. It will thus be drawn away from other organs — including the brain, which will be undersupplied with oxygen. The result: you don't feel like thinking; you become tired, sluggish, and no longer fit on the job. So an enormous lunch is neither good for you nor any help to your children; you should be alert for your afternoon responsibilities.

Nutritionists have established that small meals have a stimulating effect. For this reason you should distribute the required amount of calories over five meals a day, eating breakfast, a light morning in-between meal, lunch, an afternoon in-between meal, and supper. The brain will be kept continually supplied with energy, and blood sugar levels will be maintained. The implication for the working mother: provide for between-meal snacks which might be crispbread or whole-grain bread with cheese, yogurt, or cottage cheese with fruit or herbs. Often a handful of nuts or a few pieces of dried fruit will do. Fruit of all kinds is of course fine, but an excess of sweets is not. Sweet confections make you hungry again in a short while — just what you want to avoid.

Try not to have your evening meal too late, since a full stomach can cause sleep disturbances. For evening meals when you don't feel like cooking, be sparing with fat. Don't set out heavily buttered bread; instead, serve fresh salads, cold sliced lean meat, low-fat cheese, fruit, and whole-grain bread. Cottage cheese, especially the skim-milk type, has proved itself the ideal slenderizer.

Nutritionists have also established that people who eat five instead of three meals a day, with the same intake of calories, not only stay slim but can actually lose weight. What this boils down to is that you will weigh less with five small meals, more with three large ones. Even people who have to get meals on the table in frantic haste can set their sights accordingly — want to try it?

Buying Systematically

When you don't have much time, it is especially important to plan all purchasing meticulously and carry it out as systematically as possible. The tips I offer will help you accomplish these goals.

- The shopping list is the first priority. Never go off with the idea that "I'll think of what I need." Note down exactly what you want, also figuring items to keep stocked up on. (You'll find more on maintaining a stock of provisions on p. 7.)
- Roll-type note pads that can be attached to the kitchen wall are practical. Just as soon as an item of food runs low or is needed, it's written down so that no matter what, it won't be forgotten the next time you shop.
- Once a month you should put in a big shopping day. You can work out exactly when

according to your and your spouse's free time, but it shouldn't be on Saturdays unless there's no alternative. Late afternoons during the week are better — you'll avoid the crowds.

- Between these major shopping trips, buy especially important or perishable items (such as meat, sausage, cheese) once a week.
- The weekly meal plan is your handy helper, and if you are not a cook of shining imagination, it's an urgent necessity for simply carrying out necessary purchases. Make it out on Sunday and you'll know exactly what the course of events will be at the stove that week. Anyone who only makes out the menu the night before must have either a large stock of staples on hand or lots of time to shop.
- Yes, it's thriftier to cook in the traditional way — scrubbing vegetables, peeling and chopping onions. Unfortunately, time takes precedence over thrift in cooking on the double, so you'd better get used to buying ready-prepared foods — for example, trimmed and cut-up cabbage or soup vegetables (unless you prefer frozen or canned products). For split-second cuisine there are preboiled eggs, precooked meat patties, and a variety of other ready-made products.
- Buy salad vegetables and berries fresh every day, insofar as possible; the vitamin content declines quickly with longer storage.

Kitchen Tips for Making It Snappy

From my own bag of tricks (and that of many homemakers with careers), I've jotted down tips that might be of use to you. You may already be familiar with one or the other expedient, but it can't hurt to be reminded of them. Often one forgets one's own labor-saving discoveries.

- When you cook, always start off with whatever will take the longest. This is of course the way menus have been arranged in this book.

Saving Time in the Kitchen

- Preheat the oven or the electric stove burners as soon as you begin the preparation, so they'll be ready for the task at hand when it's time to put the pots on the stove or the baking dishes into the oven.
- Wherever boiling water is called for, start out with hot tap water. It will boil in no time at all.
- If hot liquid is used in a recipe, always put it on to heat up first thing, so as not to throw a glitch into your split-second work schedule.
- Warm up the serving dishes at the same time you start working. (Place them in the pre-heated oven — 160°-170° F/ 70°-75° C — or in very hot water.) Caution: use kitchen mitts to remove them. The exception to this rule might be if your time is so rushed that you'd just as soon have the food cool off a bit on cold plates or bowls so it's ready to eat sooner.
- Time-saving appliances like electric slicers, electric mixers, and above all the pressure cooker are indispensable for quick cuisine. Determine your needs, and equip yourself — then use these time-savers.
- Iceberg lettuce and endive are practical for split-second cooking because usually only the outer leaves have to be removed; the heads then only need to be cut or torn into smaller pieces. Rinsing is usually superfluous, since they grow so tightly packed that no grain of dirt can get in.
- Other lettuces can be cleaned and trimmed the night before. As soon as the lettuce is washed, it goes into a clear plastic bag or plastic wrap and is stored in the vegetable compartment of the refrigerator until the next day's preparations.
- Salad-making will be simplified if you have ready-made bottled dressings in the house or make up a dressing to keep on hand (recipe p. 106). Stored in a screw-top jar, it will keep about a week in the refrigerator.
- A stock of pickled delicacies (cucumbers, mixed pickles, canned pimientos or marinated bell peppers) saves you the trouble of having to make one more side dish in haste.
- Potatoes boiled in their jackets the evening before can be promptly turned into home fries the next day.
- When you want to make peeled boiled potatoes but there isn't time to peel them early in the day, peel them in the evening and let them stand, covered in cold water, in a saucepan. True, in this case you do have to accept some loss of vitamins.
- You can use garlic quickly if you press the unpeeled cloves straight into the dish through a garlic press.
- You can make rice even if you have only 10 minutes in which to cook it — because there's quick-cooking rice, which is added to boiling water and requires only 5 minutes' steeping — presto!
- Converted rice, which can be handled with never a problem because it doesn't overcook, or brown rice, which is especially healthful, can be cooked the night before, and warmed up in a colander over steaming water — it will be as good as if freshly cooked.
- Use free days that get ruined by rain, or otherwise messed up, for cooking and freezing. You'll save yourself a few days' cooking for the month, and wangle yourself a bit more free time.

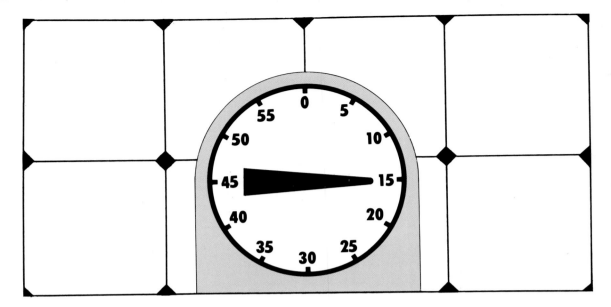

15-Minute Recipes

You probably didn't think it was possible to make a 15-minute recipe the centerpiece of a family dinner. I hope you find that this chapter proves otherwise.

There are soups, egg dishes, salads, cheese mixtures, and more. The trick in keeping the time within bounds is to rely on good ready-made accompaniments: hearty whole-grain breads from your favorite bakery, well-seasoned vegetable salads or cole slaw, spicy pickles, and relishes. Dessert is a snap with prepared products — ice cream, pudding, fruit yogurt.

Quick Goulash Soup

1 large onion

1 red or green bell pepper

2 tablespoons vegetable oil

10 oz. (300 g) ground pork or veal

1 tablespoon all-purpose flour

Pinch each of salt, paprika, and pepper

1 cup (240 ml) tomato juice

2 cups (500 ml) beef broth

1 garlic clove

1 can (16 oz./450 g) green beans

½ cup (125 ml) heavy cream

Peel and finely dice onion. Cut pepper in half and remove seeds and membranes. Rinse and quarter peppers; cut into strips.

Heat oil in saucepan large enough to hold all ingredients. Sauté diced onion until translucent. Add ground meat and sauté rapidly, stirring constantly. Sprinkle flour, salt, paprika, and pepper over meat and stir to mix well. Add strips of pepper. Gradually pour in tomato juice, then beef broth, and let soup cook 5 minutes, stirring occasionally.

Peel the garlic clove and chop coarsely. Sprinkle with a little salt and crush with fork. Drain beans in colander.

Add the garlic and beans to soup and bring to boil once more. Stir in cream and serve.

Quick Goulash Soup, easily prepared with ground pork. ▷

Menu Suggestion

Accompany with coarse sourdough rye bread or dark whole-grain pumpernickel. For dessert, stir 3 cups (700 ml) lowfat yogurt with 2 tablespoons fresh lemon juice, 2 egg yolks, and 2 tablespoons honey. Dice 4 canned peach halves and combine with the yogurt. Serve in 4 individual serving goblets and sprinkle with toasted wheat germ if desired.

Shrimp and Scrambled Eggs on Toast

1 can (5 oz./140 g) shrimp, or same amount of cooked, shelled shrimp

¼ cup (2 oz./60 g) butter

4 slices firm-textured bread

4 eggs

¼ cup (60 ml) milk

Salt and white pepper

¼ cup (60 ml) chili sauce

1 tablespoon drained capers

Drain the canned shrimp (use bulk shrimp as they are).

Melt half of butter in skillet. Sauté bread slices on both sides until golden brown. Arrange on warmed plates.

Melt remaining butter in same skillet.

Whisk eggs with milk. Season to taste with salt and white pepper. Scramble eggs in the hot butter.

Divide scrambled eggs among toast slices. Top with shrimp, chili sauce, and capers.

Variations

Ham and Eggs on Toast In 2 skillets, simultaneously sauté the bread in butter or margarine and fry the eggs sunny side up. Top each slice of bread with 2 slices of smoked ham and slide out 1 fried egg onto each serving.

Typically Danish, this open-faced Shrimp and Scrambled Egg Sandwich is served on toast.

Smoked Fish on Toast   Toast the bread slices in the toaster. Spread with 2 tablespoons (1 oz./30 g) butter or margarine. Top with trimmed smoked fish fillets (any firm-textured white fish; about 10 oz./300 g in all). Cook scrambled eggs separately, and serve with the sandwiches.

Menu Suggestion

Accompany with carrot salad mixed with apples or raisins, a beet salad (or pickled beets from your own pantry shelves), or a crisp fresh vegetable salad. Begin with oxtail soup or beef broth and finish with a fruit compote, or creamed cottage cheese blended with peach chunks, honey, cream, and fresh lemon juice.

Fried Eggs with Artichokes

1 can (8 ½ oz./240 g) canned artichoke hearts or bottoms

2 tomatoes

2 tablespoons vegetable oil

½ teaspoon salt

¼ teaspoon pepper

4 eggs

2 tablespoons heavy cream

2 tablespoons tomato paste

2 tablespoons minced fresh parsley

Drain artichokes, reserving canning liquid. Rinse and dry tomatoes; cut into slices, trimming ends.

Heat oil in skillet and sauté artichokes and sliced tomatoes over gentle heat. Combine salt and pepper; season tomato slices with half the mixture. Carefully break eggs into pan over the tomatoes, as for sunny-side-up eggs; sprinkle remaining salt and pepper over the whites and fry until crisp.

Combine cream with 1 tablespoon artichoke canning liquid, the tomato paste, and parsley. Just before serving, pour over eggs in skillet and cook until set.

A satisfying tidbit — Fried Eggs with Artichokes.

Menu Suggestion

Serve with French bread or French fries. Heat bread or frozen fries in the oven while eggs and artichokes are being prepared.

Hearty Dutch Bean Stew

2 cups (450 ml) beef broth

1 leek

1 large can (28 oz./800 g) white beans

1 small can (8 oz./225 g) carrots

8 sausages (frankfurters, bratwurst, bockwurst, or similar type; 1 ½ lb./650 g total)

1 bunch parsley

5 heaping tablespoons grated Dutch Gouda cheese

Bring broth to boil in large saucepan. Trim and wash leek, cut into rings, and simmer in broth.

Add beans and carrots (draining some of the canning liquid if desired) together with sausages. Simmer for 10 minutes, stirring occasionally.

Meanwhile, wash and mince parsley.

Stir cheese into soup. Stir in parsley. Serve soup in a tureen; arrange sausages on serving plates.

Variations

Brussels Bean Stew   Instead of carrots, simmer 1 pint (450 g) trimmed Brussels sprouts for 12 minutes in beef broth along with leek.

Provençal Bean Stew   Omit carrots and add 1 8-ounce (225 g) can peeled tomatoes instead. Use about 1 pound (450 g) smoked garlic sausage such as kielbasa. Season with *herbes de Provence* (sold ready mixed) and garlic butter. Instead of cheese, thicken the stew with 3 heaping tablespoons breadcrumbs.

Menu Suggestion

Serve with a country rye bread. For dessert, offer 8 ounces (225 g) creamed cottage cheese beaten until smooth with ¼ cup heavy cream; stir in 1 tablespoon instant coffee powder and sugar to taste.

Chinese 5-Minute Pork

¼ cup (60 ml) soy sauce

¼ cup (60 ml) dry Sherry

Salt

Pinch of sugar

4 teaspoons cornstarch

1 large piece of boneless pork tenderloin (about 1 ¼ lb./600 g)

5 tablespoons vegetable oil

8 oz. (225 g) fresh soybean sprouts

1 can (11 oz./300 g) mandarin oranges

Salad:

1 large head of lettuce

2 tablespoons vinegar

Salt, onion powder, and seasoned pepper

3 tablespoons vegetable oil

1 tablespoon chopped chives

In a bowl, combine soy sauce, Sherry, salt, sugar, and cornstarch. Cut pork tenderloin into thin slices. Toss in marinade and let stand.

Heat 3 tablespoons oil in large skillet. Sauté meat with marinade 5 minutes, stirring. Arrange on a platter and keep warm.

Quickly sauté bean sprouts in remaining oil in the same skillet. Season with salt. Arrange (along with mandarin oranges) on platter with pork.

While meat is cooking, clean and trim lettuce. Mix dressing from the remaining ingredients and toss with lettuce. Serve with the meat.

Menu Suggestion

Accompany with sweet and sour pickled vegetables or mango chutney, fluffy white rice or French bread. For dessert, serve vanilla fudge ice cream.

Chinese 5-Minute Pork is a light and nutritious meal. ▷

Corned Beef and Egg on Toast

4 slices firm-textured white bread

2 tablespoons (1 oz./30 g) butter

4 eggs

Salt

4 slices corned beef (about 1 lb./400 g total)

1 small bottle (3 oz./85 g) capers

8 anchovy fillets, packed in oil

Toast the bread and distribute on 4 plates.

Melt butter in large skillet. Break eggs into skillet and fry sunny side up. Salt lightly.

Divide corned beef among toast slices and slide the eggs on top.

Drain capers; garnish sandwiches with the capers and 2 anchovy fillets each.

Variation

Grilled Ham and Cheese with Fried Eggs and Shrimp   Preheat broiler. Place 4 slices light rye or wholewheat bread on broiler rack, topping them with 1 slice each boiled ham and Edam cheese. Broil until cheese begins to melt. Meanwhile, fry 4 eggs sunny side up; salt lightly. Drain 1 can (2½ oz./70 g) shrimp. Distribute fried eggs over the sandwiches, topping with shrimp. Sprinkle generously with chopped chives.

Menu Suggestion

Begin with chicken broth. With the sandwiches, serve a potato or celery root salad; for dessert, vanilla pudding with raspberry syrup or chocolate sauce.

Corned Beef and Egg on Toast, just as the English like it. . . and sure to please your palate as well.

Scrambled Eggs and Salami on Toast

1 can (8 oz./230 g) mushrooms

2 tablespoons (1 oz./30 g) margarine or butter

4 eggs

¼ cup (60 ml) evaporated milk

Salt and pepper

2 tablespoons minced fresh parsley

4 slices firm-textured bread

1 tomato

16 slices salami (use mild or cotto type, not hard)

Drain mushrooms. Melt margarine in skillet.

Beat eggs with evaporated milk, salt, pepper, and 1½ tablespoons parsley. Stir in mushrooms.

Pour mixture into skillet and cook, scrambling the eggs.

Toast bread in the toaster.

Rinse and dry tomato; cut into 4 slices.

Top toast slices with 4 slices of salami each. Divide scrambled egg mixture over the salami. Top with tomato slices. Serve sprinkled with remaining parsley.

Variation

Fried Egg and Bologna Sandwiches   Spread 4 slices coarse whole-grain bread with butter and top each with 2 slices good-quality bologna. Place 1 fried egg on each sandwich. Sprinkle with minced chives.

Menu Suggestion

Accompany with sliced tomatoes seasoned with salt, white pepper, and onion powder. Set vinegar and oil on the table for dressing. You might also serve marinated vegetables (for example, sweet peppers or mushrooms). Afterwards try fruit yogurt or a cottage cheese-fruit combination. Fresh fruit would be good, too — apples or oranges, peaches or apricots.

Scrambled Eggs and Salami on Toast, protein-rich and appetite satisfying.

Cheese Soup with Small Beef Balls

Beef balls:

1 onion

10 oz. (300 g) chopped lean beef sirloin

1 small egg or ½ large egg

Salt and seasoned pepper

Soup:

¼ cup (2 oz./60 g) butter or margarine

3 tablespoons all-purpose flour

4 cups (950 ml) hot beef broth

1 package (10 oz./300 g) frozen tiny peas

4 oz. (125 g) processed cheese, preferably herb-flavored

2 tablespoons chopped chives

Peel and chop onion. In a bowl, combine onion with beef, egg, and seasonings to form a smooth-textured mixture. Season to taste and shape into small oval balls.

Melt butter or margarine in soup kettle. Stir in flour and cook over low heat to make a roux. Stir in broth. Bring to boil and add peas; simmer 5 minutes. Slice or break cheese into the soup in small bits and stir until it melts.

Add meatballs to the soup, and cook 5 minutes at a bare simmer. Stir in chives. Serve soup in warmed soup plates or cups.

Variations

Cheese Soup with Sausage Balls   Instead of chopped beef, use 10 ounces (300 g) fresh pork sausage mixture. Simply work in 1 egg and shape small balls from the mixture with a teaspoon.

Cheese Soup with Cocktail Sausages   Instead of the peas, add 1 can (8 oz./225 g) drained green beans to soup along with 4 cocktail sausages per serving. Season to taste with fresh savory, though minced parsley is very good too.

Time Tip When you are preparing soup, you should always heat the broth or stock in advance. Put it on just as soon as you start your cooking preparations, and it will be hot when you need it.

Spiked Sausage Kebabs

4 frankfurters (about 8 to 10 oz./225 to 280 g total)

4 slices canned pineapple

1 tablespoon (½ oz./15 g) butter or margarine (for baking dish)

¼ cup (60 ml) Danish akvavit

1 tablespoon curry powder

8 slices Danish Havarti cheese (about 5 oz./160 g total)

8 thin slices Danish-style bacon or streaky smoked bacon (about 3 oz./80 g total)

1 bunch parsley

Heat electric broiler or oven broiling unit.

Cut frankfurters and pineapple slices into 4 pieces each. Skewer on 4 cocktail skewers, alternating sausage and pineapple.

Butter ovenproof dish and lay skewers in it. Drizzle with akvavit. Sprinkle curry powder over kebabs and top with slices of Havarti cheese.

Toast under preheated broiler 8 to 10 minutes or until the cheese melts.

Meanwhile, fry bacon in ungreased skillet until crisp. Garnish the finished dish with bacon and rinsed and dried parsley sprigs.

Menu Suggestion

Begin with cream of tomato soup. With the sausage kebabs, have ketchup and bread or rolls.

◄ Cheese Soup with Small Beef Balls, enriched further with peas and fresh herbs.

Country-Style Eggs

3 tablespoons (1 ½ oz./45 g) butter or margarine

*16 slices (7 oz./200 g total) salami
(use mild or cotto type, not hard)*

¼ cup (60 ml) chopped chives

8 eggs

Mild Hungarian paprika

Salt and white pepper

Adjust rack to top of oven and preheat oven to 400°F (200°C).
   Grease large rimmed ovenproof platter with half the butter or margarine. Line platter with the salami slices. Sprinkle with chives.
   Carefully break eggs over the salami. Season with paprika, a little salt, and white pepper. Dot tops of eggs with remaining butter or margarine.
   Bake 5 minutes or until eggs are set.

Variations

Salami and Cheese Eggs   Grease ovenproof platter. Line with buttered slices of firm-textured bread (homemade type, suitable for toasting). Distribute salami slices, chives, and 8 slices of Edam cheese over the bread. Bake as above. Fry the eggs separately.

Bologna-Cheese Bake   Grease ovenproof platter. Line with 7 ounces (200 g) sliced good-quality bologna, mortadella, or other mild sausage. Distribute drained canned mushrooms over bologna and top with slices of Tilsit or Havarti cheese. Scatter some chopped chives over the cheese and bake as above.

Scrambled Eggs and Cheese on Ham   Finely dice 4 ounces (100 g) Bel Paese cheese. Beat 8 eggs. Stir in cheese. Season with salt and white pepper to taste.
   Stir in 2 ounces (50 g) grated Parmesan cheese. Melt 2 tablespoons margarine in large skillet and scramble egg and cheese mixture over low heat until set. Toast 8 slices firm bread in the toaster; butter

lightly. Distribute 1 slice of boiled ham and some of the scrambled egg mixture over each slice of toast. Sprinkle with mild Hungarian paprika and serve at once. Sliced tomatoes are a good accompaniment (let everyone season them at table according to preference).

Menu Suggestion
Accompany with cole slaw or red pepper salad, along with country-style rye bread. For dessert, serve seasonal fresh fruit or a fruit compote.

Whipped Cheese with Strawberries

1 pint (340 g) fresh small strawberries

*1 lb. (450 g) creamed cottage cheese or mixture of
   half fresh farmer cheese and half cream cheese,
   sieved and beaten smooth*

Pinch of cinnamon

1 tablespoon sugar

Rinse strawberries under cold water, drain and hull. Leave whole or halve as you prefer.
   Flavor cheese with cinnamon. Distribute on 4 plates and arrange strawberries on each. Sprinkle with sugar.

Variations
Strawberry Whip   Quarter the strawberries and combine with 3 tablespoons sugar. Beat ½ cup (125 ml) heavy cream into the cheese. Combine strawberries and cheese.

Peach-Ginger Whip   Peel, halve, and pit 4 large peaches. Cut into slices. Combine with 3 tablespoons sugar. Flavor with ½ teaspoon ground ginger. Stir into the cheese.

Menu Suggestion
For the main course, offer a hearty one-dish stew, served with wholewheat bread.

Country-Style Eggs are baked in the oven.

Creamed Fruit Cocktail

1 can (16 oz./450 g) fruit cocktail

1 cup (240 ml) heavy cream

1 lb. (450 g) creamed cottage cheese or mixture of half fresh farmer cheese and half cream cheese, sieved and beaten smooth

2 tablespoons sugar

Pinch of ground ginger

¼ cup (60 ml) framboise (raspberry eau de vie)

Drain fruit cocktail. Whip cream until stiff.
Combine cheese with the sugar and flavor with the ginger. Add raspberry *eau de vie.*
Combine fruit cocktail and cream with cheese and arrange on 4 plates. Chill lightly before serving.

Variations

Banana-Orange Cocktail Peel and dice 1 banana and 1 orange. Sweeten lightly with sugar. In place of fruit cocktail, add banana and orange to the flavored cheese and cream mixture.

Chocolate Cocktail Combine 1 pound (450 g) cheese with ½ can (11 oz./300 g) drained mandarin orange segments. Fold in 3 tablespoons chocolate sauce. Flavor generously with ginger. Divide among 4 plates. Sprinkle with coarsely grated semisweet chocolate.

Zesty Cottage Cheese with Apples

1 large onion

2 tart apples

1 lb. (450 g) cottage cheese, or half cottage cheese and half cream cheese beaten together

1 cup (240 ml) heavy cream

½ teaspoon salt

Zesty Cottage Cheese with Apples is piquant with the flavor of onions.

Peel onion and slice very thinly. Rinse, dry, and quarter the apples (do not peel); core them and shred coarsely.

Place cheese in large bowl and beat with cream until smooth. Stir in onion and apples and season with salt.

Savory Cottage Cheese

8 oz. (225 g) cottage cheese, or half cottage cheese, and half cream cheese beaten together

5 tablespoons milk

1 small red bell pepper

1 medium-size sweet pickle

1 very small onion

½ bunch radishes

Pinch of salt

A few drops of hot pepper sauce

In a bowl large enough to hold all ingredients, beat cheese with milk until smooth.

Halve pepper and remove seeds and membranes. Rinse pepper, drain, and dice finely. Finely dice pickle. Peel and finely chop onion. Rinse radishes and cut into small dice.

Stir diced pepper, pickle, onion, and radishes into the cheese. Season to taste with salt and hot pepper sauce.

Raspberry—Nut Snack

1 pint (340 g) fresh raspberries

2 tablespoons orange juice

1 tablespoon honey

8 oz. (225 g) cottage cheese

2 tablespoons milk

1 tablespoon sugar

¼ cup (30 g) chopped almonds

Savory Cottage Cheese is a zesty spread for bread.

Rinse and hull strawberries; halve and set aside 12 especially pretty berries. Puree remaining berries in blender with orange juice and honey.

Beat cheese with milk and sugar; lightly fold in strawberry puree.

Spoon into globlets, garnish with halved strawberries, and scatter 1 tablespoon almonds over each serving.

Camembert Snacks with Pineapple

1 Camembert cheese (9 oz./250 g)

1 teaspoon hot prepared mustard

2 thick slices boiled ham (4 oz./100 g total)

2 tablespoons vegetable oil

1 egg

2 tablespoons all-purpose flour

2 tablespoons breadcrumbs

1 teaspoon butter

2 slices canned pineapple

Parsley sprigs

Cut Camembert into 8 slices, each about ⅜ inch (1 cm) thick. Spread one side with mustard. Cut each ham slice in two; the pieces should be the same size as the Camembert slices. Place ham over 4 slices of cheese and place remaining cheese slices on top; mustard side should be next to the ham. Press together firmly.

Rapidly heat the oil in skillet. Beat egg in a deep plate. Arrange flour and breadcrumbs on 2 more plates.

Dip cheese-ham sandwiches first in flour, then egg, then breadcrumbs. Press breading lightly to make it adhere.

Fry the breaded "sandwiches" on both sides over high heat for 2 to 3 minutes. Melt butter in small skillet. Drain canned pineapple slices, and cut in half. Sauté in the butter until lightly browned. Arrange on plates with Camembert and garnish with parsley.

Menu Suggestion

Begin with cream of mushroom soup. With the Camembert, serve dark whole-grain bread or light rye (or wholewheat) bread and Cumberland sauce.

Hot and Sour Soup with Fruit Kebabs

2 ½ cups (600 ml) cold water

1 quart (1 L) Chinese hot and sour soup (from takeout restaurant) or 1 packet (1.41 oz./40 g) Chinese egg flower soup mix

½ medium banana

4 canned sour cherries

4 canned mandarin orange segments

1 tablespoon coarsely chopped almonds

Place hot and sour soup in saucepan and keep hot over low heat. If using egg flower soup mix, prepare according to package directions.

Meanwhile, peel banana and cut into 4 chunks. Slide first the sour cherries, then the mandarin segments, then the banana slices onto 4 cocktail skewers.

Distribute soup in 4 soup cups; sprinkle with chopped almonds. Place 1 fruit kebab in each cup.

Menu Suggestion

Begin with Waldorf salad, homemade or purchased. With the soup, serve bread and butter with slices of ham or cold cuts. Afterwards, serve chocolate pudding or seasonal fresh fruit, and fortune cookies or Chinese almond cookies.

◁ A skillet surprise — Camembert Snacks with Pineapple.

Hungarian Beef Salad

I suggest you cook the beef — and, for the sake of practicality, also boil the eggs for the garnish — the night before. You can also buy ready-cooked beef brisket.

1 lb (450 g) lean boiled beef

4 sweet or sour pickles

1 large green bell pepper

2 tomatoes

Dressing:

1 tablespoon wine vinegar

Pinch of sugar

Cayenne pepper and seasoned salt

1 onion

3 tablespoons vegetable oil

1 tablespoon minced fresh parsley

2 hard-cooked eggs

1 small bunch parsley

Cut beef and pickles into strips.

Quarter green pepper and remove seeds; rinse pepper and cut into strips. Rinse and dice the tomatoes.

For the dressing, whisk vinegar in a bowl with sugar, a little cayenne pepper, and salt. Peel and chop onion; add to vinegar mixture. Season to taste. Stir in oil and parsley. Fold beef, pickles, green pepper, and tomatoes into the dressing. Season to taste and arrange for serving. Garnish with the eggs (cut into eighths) and parsley.

Variation

Salade à l'Hongroise The genuine *salade à l'hongroise* should also include about 10 ounces (300 g) shredded cabbage (pour boiling water over to wilt it first) and 4 ounces (100 g) bacon, fried and diced.

Hungarian Beef Salad has a piquant combination of sweet pickles, green peppers, and tomatoes.

Endive and Cucumber Salad

3 Belgian endives

1 medium cucumber

2 tablespoons wine vinegar

Salt and white pepper

1 teaspoon dry English mustard or prepared hot mustard

Pinch of sugar

Garlic powder

1 tablespoon chili sauce

3 tablespoons vegetable oil

Rinse endives; remove any withered leaves. Cut away about ⅜ inch (1 cm) from stem ends and lift out the whole leaves. Rinse only if necessary. Cut endive leaves into pieces about ¾ inch (2 cm) long.

Rinse and dry cucumber; do not peel. Cut into paper-thin slices. Combine cut-up endive and sliced cucumber.

For the dressing, whisk vinegar with salt, pepper, mustard, sugar, and garlic powder. Add chili sauce and season to taste. Stir in oil.

Arrange salad in a bowl. Pour dressing into the center and toss at the table.

Variation

Fruited Endive and Cucumber Salad In addition to the above ingredients, mix in 1 can (11 oz./300 g) drained mandarin oranges. Flavor the dressing with 1 tablespoon currant jelly, 1 tablespoon grated horse-radish, a little fresh lemon juice, ¼ teaspoon ground ginger, and salt to taste. Stir in ¼ cup heavy cream.

Menu Suggestion

Serve as accompaniment to beef filet steaks and mashed potatoes or rice. For dessert, serve vanilla ice cream.

Endive and Cucumber Salad is an excellent accompaniment to broiled meats.

20-Minute Recipes

Beefburgers with Fried Eggs

3 tablespoons (1 ½ oz./45 g) herbed butter

1 package (1 lb./450 g) frozen beef patties

4 small onions

2 tablespoons (1 oz./30 g) margarine or butter

4 eggs

Salt and white pepper

1 tablespoon chopped chives

Melt herbed butter in skillet and sauté burgers over low heat, 3 minutes per side.

Meanwhile, peel onions and cut into rings. Sauté along with the burgers another 5 minutes.

Melt margarine in another large skillet. Fry the eggs sunny side up. Season the egg whites with salt, the yolks with white pepper.

Arrange burgers on 4 warmed plates. Divide onions over them and slide 1 fried egg onto each. Serve sprinkled with chives.

Time Tip Of course, the time will be too short to boil potatoes, but there are tricks. You can boil potatoes in their jackets the night before, peel them, and cut into slices ready to be fried at the same time as the beefburgers. Or use canned potatoes.

Spaghetti L'Amatriciana

4 oz. (125 g) streaky bacon

2 tablespoons olive oil

1 small onion

1 small hot pepper

1 can (16 oz./450 g) peeled tomatoes

Salt

1 lb. (450 g) spaghetti

3 oz. (75 g) coarsely grated pecorino cheese

◄ Beefburgers with Fried Eggs — a quick meal.

In large saucepan bring a large amount of water to boil for the spaghetti. Dice the bacon. Heat olive oil in heavy saucepan and cook bacon in the oil until fat is rendered.

Peel and dice onion. Seed the hot pepper. Remove bacon from the pan. Sauté diced onion and pepper in bacon fat. Add tomatoes. Stir thoroughly and simmer, uncovered, 10 minutes over moderate heat.

Salt the boiling water; add the spaghetti. Cook *al dente* (12 to 15 minutes), drain, and briefly rinse under cold water. Transfer to warmed bowl or individual plates.

Remove pepper from the sauce; add the diced bacon. Season to taste. Spoon sauce over pasta and sprinkle with grated pecorino cheese.

Spaghetti with Sauce alla Romana

1 lb. (450 g) spaghetti

Salt

1 tablespoon olive oil

1 small onion

1 garlic clove

8 oz. (250 g) mixed ground meat (beef, pork, and veal)

10 oz. (300 g) canned peeled tomatoes

Salt and pepper

Pinch of sugar

1 teaspoon dried basil

1 bay leaf

20 pimiento-stuffed olives

In a large saucepan, bring a large amount of water to boil. Add spaghetti and salt and cook *al dente* (just firm to the bite), 12 to 15 minutes. Drain, briefly rinse under cold water, and allow to drain thoroughly. Transfer to warmed serving dish.

Meanwhile, heat oil in skillet. Peel and chop onion and garlic and sauté until golden in the oil. Add chopped meat and sauté rapidly. Add tomatoes and heat the mixture and season with salt, pepper, sugar, basil, and bay leaf. Simmer 15 minutes.

Cut olives in half and add to sauce. Heat 5 minutes. Remove bay leaf. Adjust seasoning of sauce and serve over the pasta.

Menu Suggestion

Follow with seasonal fruits and yogurt, or make a mocha cottage cheese whip. Just whip 8 ounces (250 g) cottage cheese (or mixture of cream cheese and fresh farmer cheese) with 2 teaspoons vanilla sugar (or ½ teaspoon vanilla extract), 1 tablespoon instant coffee powder, 1 cup (240 ml) heavy cream, a pinch of salt, and 5 tablespoons sugar.

> **Cooking Tip** 1 teaspoon of oil added to the cooking water will keep pasta from sticking together.

Pasta with Chicken Livers

10 oz. (300 g) fettuccine or other flat noodles

Salt

1 small onion

1 garlic clove

2 slices streaky bacon

2 tablespoons vegetable oil

1 medium-size green bell pepper

8 oz. (250 g) chicken livers

10 oz. (270 g) canned peeled tomatoes

½ cup (125 ml) dry white wine

White pepper

1 teaspoon mild Hungarian paprika

4 oz. (100 g) grated Gouda cheese, preferably medium-aged

Spaghetti with Sauce alla Romana, a taste of Italian cuisine. ▷

Bring large amount of water to boil. Add noodles and salt and cook *al dente* (12 to 15 minutes). Drain and briefly rinse under cold water. Drain thoroughly. Transfer to warmed serving dish.

Meanwhile, dice peeled onion and garlic and the bacon. Heat oil in skillet. Sauté bacon in oil until translucent. Add onion and garlic and cook until golden.

Rinse green pepper and cut in half. Remove core and seeds and chop pepper coarsely. Briefly rinse the chicken livers under cold water, blot dry on paper towels and cut into slices. Sauté quickly for 3 minutes. Add tomatoes, pouring off some of the liquid. Pour in wine. Heat, add pepper and paprika, and adjust seasoning. Stir in Gouda cheese and serve over hot noodles.

Menu Suggestion

Begin with a canned soup of your choice. With the noodles, serve a tomato salad.

Toasted Ham-and-Cheese Sandwiches with Apple Slices

1 medium apple

3 tablespoons (1 ½ oz./45 g) butter

4 slices firm-textured bread

4 slices boiled ham (5 oz./150 g total)

8 slices American or Cheddar cheese

Rinse, dry, and core the apple. Cut in 8 thin or 4 thicker slices.

Melt 2 tablespoons (1 oz./30 g) butter in large skillet. Over low heat, sauté bread on one side until crisp. At the same time, sauté ham slices on both sides. Remove bread and ham from skillet.

Melt remaining butter in same skillet and sauté apple slices until golden. Remove from skillet. Return bread slices to skillet; top with ham slices, then the cheese. Cover tightly, and cook until cheese is melted and light brown (about 5 minutes). Serve garnished with apple slices.

Menu Suggestion

Begin with bean soup. With the sandwiches, serve a salad of sweet peppers or mixed vegetables. Offer sherbet or a frozen parfait for dessert.

Potato Frittata

1 ½ lb. (680 g) canned or cooked peeled potatoes

5 to 6 slices streaky bacon (5 oz./150 g)

2 tablespoons (1 oz./30 g) margarine or butter

Salt

4 eggs

¼ cup (60 ml) milk

White pepper

1 bunch chives

Turn potatoes into a colander. Wipe dry with paper towels; cut into slices. Cut bacon into strips and fry until golden brown in large skillet. Add margarine and let melt.

Add sliced potatoes; salt lightly if necessary. Sauté in bacon fat over high heat 10 minutes, or until golden brown, turning occasionally.

Meanwhile, beat eggs with milk; season with a little salt and freshly ground white pepper. Pour over potatoes. Cook over high heat until set, at least 5 minutes, covering skillet if necessary. Wash and mince chives and sprinkle over the dish, which should be served straight from the skillet.

Variations

Potato-Cheese Frittata   Prepare this as directed above, adding 4 ounces (100 g) Edam cheese. The minced chives can be added to the egg mixture.

Potato-Seafood Frittata   Combine 5 to 7 ounces (150 to 200 g) canned shrimp or bits of smoked fish with the egg mixture. Use dill instead of chives.

Menu Suggestion

As a side dish, make a salad from 1 small can (5 ¼ oz./150 g) corn, 2 tomatoes cut into eighths, 1 small can (6 oz./175 g) green beans (or frozen green beans cooked according to package directions) and fresh-cut onion rings. Make a dressing of vinegar, oil, salt, seasoned pepper, and onion powder. Stir in 1 egg yolk and combine with the rest of the salad ingredients. For dessert, serve chocolate pudding with a vanilla custard sauce.

Potato Frittata is a bonus for anyone who has to cook on the double.   ▷

20-Minute Recipes

Shrimp with Scrambled Eggs

1 lb. (450 g) shelled shrimp

2 slices streaky bacon

1 onion

2 medium-size boiled potatoes (cooked the day before)

2 tablespoons vegetable oil

½ teaspoon salt

1 teaspoon white pepper

3 eggs

3 tablespoons heavy cream

1 tablespoon dried dillweed

2 slices firm-textured bread

3 tablespoons (1 ½ oz./45 g) butter

Turn shrimp into colander, rinse with cold water, and drain. Finely dice bacon. Peel and dice onion. Peel potatoes and cut into thin slices (this takes practically no time with an egg slicer).

Heat oil in skillet. Fry diced bacon in oil until crisp. Add diced onion and cook until translucent but not brown. Stir in sliced potatoes, add drained shrimp and sauté, tossing constantly.

Beat salt, pepper, eggs, cream, and dill with a whisk and pour over contents of skillet. Scramble over gentle heat until egg mixture begins to set.

Cut bread into cubes and butter into small pieces. Scatter both over the shrimp-egg mixture and give everything one more stir.

Variation

Sweet and Sour Shrimp with Eggs   Make this dish more piquant by adding sweet and sour pickles or dill pickles, cut into small bits and combined with the shrimp. Substitute chives for the dill if you wish.

Menu Suggestion

Begin with small servings of beef broth whisked with plenty of minced fresh parsley. With the shrimp and scrambled eggs, serve pickled beets. For dessert, offer a banana milk shake — made in the blender and enriched with several tablespoons of heavy cream.

Mini-Cheeseburgers on Toast

1 onion

8 oz. (225 g) chopped lean beef sirloin

1 small egg or ½ large egg

Salt and seasoned pepper

4 slices firm-textured bread

2 tablespoons (1 oz./30 g) butter or margarine

2 tablespoons ketchup

8 slices American or Cheddar cheese

4 parsley sprigs

Peel and mince onion. Place in a bowl with chopped meat; add egg, salt, and seasoned pepper. Work until smooth and season to taste (mixture should be quite flavorful). Divide over bread slices.

Melt butter or margarine in large skillet and sauté the sandwiches, meat side down, 6 minutes. Turn. Spread with ketchup and top with cheese slices.

Continue to cook in tightly covered skillet over moderate heat until cheese melts, about 5 minutes.

Arrange cheeseburgers on warmed plates. Distribute remaining ketchup over them. Garnish with parsley.

Variation

Sausageburgers   Use fresh pork sausage mixture instead of chopped beef. Spread with barbecue sauce, and proceed as above. For the final garnish use barbecue sauce and chives.

Menu Suggestion

Begin with chicken noodle soup. With the cheeseburgers, serve sliced tomatoes. Have vinegar, oil, and seasonings on the table for diners to dress salads. For dessert, serve cookies or brownies.

Quick Chicken Fricassee

1 ½ cups (350 ml) chicken broth

1 poached or broiled chicken, about 2 lb. (1 kg)

¼ cup (2 oz./60 g) butter or margarine

1 small onion

¼ cup (30 g) all-purpose flour

1 bunch parsley

Garden cress or other fresh greens or herbs

Salt and white pepper

Juice of ½ lemon

½ cup (125 ml) heavy cream

1 egg yolk

8 oz. (200 g) canned asparagus tips

Freshly grated nutmeg

Heat chicken broth in saucepan.

Skin the chicken. Remove meat from bones and cut into even-sized pieces.

Melt butter or margarine in a second saucepan. Peel and chop onion and sauté in butter until translucent; do not brown.

Stir in flour and cook to make a roux. Stir in hot chicken broth. Add rinsed parsley (setting aside several sprigs for garnish) and cress. Season with salt and pepper. Heat until warmed through, about 3 minutes. Press sauce through a sieve. Pour into saucepan; add chicken pieces and heat. Stir in lemon juice.

Whisk cream with egg yolk and stir into the fricassee. Fold in drained asparagus tips and heat, but do not allow to boil again. Flavor with nutmeg and adjust the seasoning. Transfer to serving dish. Chop remaining parsley and sprinkle over top.

Variation

Chicken Fricassee with Artichokes   In addition to the other ingredients, fold in 1 can (6 oz./175 g) drained artichoke hearts or use 1 package (10 oz./300 g) frozen hearts.

Quick Chicken Fricassee is a tasty dish for all who watch their figure.

Menu Suggestion

As a side dish, offer fluffy white rice with chopped parsley, and sliced tomatoes seasoned with salt, pepper and lemon juice. For dessert, serve cherry pie.

Dutch Fish Ragout

1 ¾ lbs. (800 g) codfish fillets

Juice of 1 lemon

Salt

4 oz. (100 g) Gouda cheese, preferably medium-aged

3 tablespoons (1 ½ oz./45 g) butter or margarine

2 tablespoons all-purpose flour

1 cup (240 ml) milk

1 teaspoon instant beef broth

2 egg yolks

½ cup (125 ml) dry white wine

Freshly grated nutmeg

White pepper

1 bunch dill

Briefly rinse codfish fillets under cold water. Allow to drain on paper towels. Cut into large, even-sized cubes. Sprinkle with lemon juice and marinate, covered, on a platter.

Bring about ½ cup (125 ml) water to boil; add salt. Poach fish with the water at a bare simmer for about 8 minutes (allow 9 minutes per inch of thickness of fish).

Meanwhile, coarsely shred cheese.

Melt butter or margarine in saucepan. Stir in flour and cook to make a roux. Stir in milk and cook 2 minutes. Add broth base and cheese and cook to dissolve broth, stirring. Carefully fold in fish cubes

Dutch Fish Ragout is enriched with medium-aged Gouda cheese.

with their poaching liquid. Cook at a bare simmer another 5 minutes.

Whisk egg yolks. Stir a little of the hot sauce into yolks, then return to ragout, and heat but do not boil. Add white wine. Season generously with nutmeg and white pepper. Rinse the dill, chop coarsely, and stir in. Serve in a warmed dish.

Boiled Eggs in Sauce Mornay

8 eggs

3 tablespoons (1 ½ oz./45g) butter or margarine

1 onion

2 tablespoons all-purpose flour

1 cup (240 ml) hot beef broth

½ cup (125 ml) milk

Salt and white pepper

3 heaping tablespoons grated Parmesan cheese

3 tablespoons grated Swiss cheese

2 egg yolks

½ cup (125 ml) heavy cream

Freshly grated nutmeg

½ bunch parsley

Place eggs in boiling water and cook until medium-boiled, 5 minutes.

Melt 1 tablespoon (½ oz./15 g) butter or margarine in a saucepan.

Peel and finely chop onion. Add to margarine and sauté until light golden.

Stir in flour and cook to make a roux. Stir in hot beef broth and cook to heat through, 2 minutes. Press through sieve or food mill.

Add milk, heat the mixture, and season with salt and pepper. Add grated cheese and remaining butter and stir until cheese melts. Whisk egg yolks with cream and stir into the sauce; heat, but do not boil. Season to taste with nutmeg.

Arrange shelled and halved eggs in the sauce. Rinse and chop parsley and scatter it over the dish.

Menu Suggestion

Begin with a hearty beef broth. With the eggs, serve French bread. For dessert, offer canned apricots or an orange dessert made from 2 oranges, peeled, divided into segments and diced (seeds removed), then combined with 4 teaspoons superfine sugar. Divide among 4 dessert plates. Whisk ¼ cup prepared eggnog with 1 teaspoon instant coffee powder and drizzle over the diced oranges.

> **Time Tip** Grate or shred cheese a few hours in advance. Store grated cheese in screw-top jars and keep them in the refrigerator.

Calves' Liver with Raisins and Almonds

12 oz. (350 g) calves' liver

3 tablespoons all-purpose flour

3 tablespoons vegetable oil

2 tablespoons (1 ½ oz./45 g) butter

1 teaspoon salt

½ teaspoon pepper

2 teaspoons instant chicken or beef broth

3 tablespoons light raisins

¼ cup (60 ml) Madeira

*½ teaspoon bottled garlic juice or
1 small garlic clove, peeled and minced*

¼ cup (30 g) slivered almonds

½ bunch parsley

4 slices firmed-textured bread

Blot liver dry with paper towels, then cut into strips. Place flour in a deep plate and toss liver strips in it. Heat oil in skillet. Briskly sauté liver strips over high heat, tossing, then remove from skillet.

Combine pan drippings with butter, salt, pepper, broth base, raisins, Madeira, and garlic juice and allow the mixture to simmer 5 minutes.

Return liver strips to skillet and cook until done, another 2 minutes. Add slivered almonds.

Rinse the parsley, blot dry, and mince.

Distribute liver mixture over the slices of bread and sprinkle with parsley.

Pasta with Egg and Parsley Sauce

1 lb. (450 g) spaghetti or linguine

1 large bunch parsley

6 eggs

Salt and freshly ground pepper

2 tablespoons grated pecorino cheese

2 tablespoons bacon drippings

1 tablespoon (½ oz./15 g) butter

Cook the pasta *al dente.*

Meanwhile, rinse and finely chop parsley. Combine in a bowl with eggs, salt, plenty of pepper, and the cheese; beat well.

Heat bacon drippings with butter in flameproof serving dish. Keep warm over very gentle heat.

Drain the pasta, saving ¼ cup of the cooking water and adding this to the fat along with the pasta. Combine thoroughly. Pour egg and cheese mixture over the pasta and stir until eggs just begin to thicken. Serve at once, with peppermill at hand.

Pasta with Anchovies

1 lb. (450 g) spaghetti or linguine

2 garlic cloves

1 bunch parsley

12 to 15 anchovy fillets

1 tablespoon vegetable oil

Freshly ground pepper

Cook the pasta *al dente.*

Meanwhile, peel and mince garlic cloves. Rinse and mince parsley. Mash anchovies with fork.

Heat oil in small skillet. Briefly sauté the garlic; do not let it color. Add parsley and anchovies and cook at a bare simmer for 2 to 3 minutes. Remove from heat and season to taste with freshly ground pepper.

Drain pasta. Save ¼ cup of the cooking water and thin the anchovy sauce with it.

Turn pasta out into a flameproof serving dish and pour sauce over it. Let it simmer a moment over the lowest possible heat, stirring constantly. Serve at once.

Spaghetti with Tomato and Basil Sauce

2 to 3 garlic cloves

1 can (16 oz./450 g) tomatoes

6 anchovy fillets

1 bunch basil

¼ cup (60 ml) olive oil

1 small peperoncino (hot pepper)

1 lb. (450 g) spaghetti

1 teaspoon vegetable oil

Peel garlic cloves. Pour canned tomatoes into a colander; drain and lightly chop or crush.

Mince anchovies. Rinse the basil; strip leaves from stems and chop.

Gently heat oil in skillet and sauté garlic cloves until they turn brown; discard garlic.

Add peperoncino and anchovies to skillet and stir until the anchovies disintegrate, then discard the peperoncino.

Add chopped tomatoes and basil leaves to skillet and simmer, covered, 14 minutes over low heat.

Meanwhile, cook paste *al dente,* with 1 teaspoon oil in the cooking water. Drain (do not rinse) and serve hot with the sauce.

A delicious summer meal: Spaghetti with Tomato and Basil Sauce.   ▶

Veal Cutlets with Mushroom Sauce

4 veal cutlets (7 oz./200 g each)

1 tablespoon vegetable oil

2 cans (8 oz./225 g each) mushrooms

2 tablespoons (1 oz./30 g) butter

Salt and white pepper

Garlic powder

1 scant cup (200 ml) Port

Preheat electric broiler or oven broiling unit.

Brush veal cutlets with oil. Score any fatty edges on the meat. Broil the cutlets 4 minutes on each side.

Meanwhile, drain mushrooms, reserving canning liquid. Melt butter and rapidly sauté the mushrooms. Season to taste with salt, white pepper, and garlic powder. Add the Port, and boil for a minute or two; pour in a little of the canning liquid if you like.

Season cutlets with salt and pepper. Arrange on warmed plates and distribute the mushrooms on top. Accompany with rice or Italian bread.

Soup with Roquefort Snacks

1 can (10 ½ oz./300 g) vegetable soup

4 ounces (100 g) Roquefort cheese

5 tablespoons (2 ½ oz./75 g) butter

8 slices pumpernickel bread

8 pimiento-stuffed olives

Freshly grated nutmeg

½ bunch parsley

Heat soup in saucepan according to directions on can.

Cream Roquefort and butter in small bowl. Spread on pumpernickel slices. Cut each slice in half

Quickly made with canned mushrooms — Veal Cutlets with Mushroom Sauce.

lengthwise. Place slices over each other, two by two, with cheese side facing up.

Cut olives into slices. Garnish each "sandwich" with olive slices. Arrange on 4 large plates. Season soup to taste with nutmeg. Divide among 4 soup cups and place on serving plates. Garnish with parsley.

Veal Cutlets with Ginger-Pepper Sauce

4 veal cutlets (7 oz./200 g each)

1 tablespoon vegetable oil

1 onion

2 tablespoons (1 oz./30 g) margarine or butter

1 tablespoon all-purpose flour

1 small jar (2 oz./70 g) sliced pimientos

½ cup (125 ml) beef broth

Salt and white pepper

1 tablespoon syrup from candied ginger

1 large piece candied ginger in syrup, drained

8 shelled walnuts

4 lettuce leaves

1 jar (4 oz./120 g) pimientos or mild cherry peppers

Preheat electric broiler or oven broiling unit.

Brush veal cutlets with oil. Broil 4 minutes on each side. Meanwhile, peel and chop onion. Melt margarine in saucepan; sauté onion. Stir in flour and cook to make a roux; stir in diced pimientos. Add beef broth and cook 2 minutes, stirring. Season with salt, white pepper, and ginger syrup.

Chop ginger and walnuts. Salt and pepper the cutlets on both sides; spread with pepper sauce. Arrange on serving plates and divide chopped ginger and walnuts over cutlets. Garnish with lettuce leaves and a few pieces of tomato pepper. Serve remaining tomato peppers on the side.

Something out of the ordinary, even for guests with pampered palates: Veal Cutlets with Ginger-Pepper Sauce. 41

Barbecued Sausages

4 knackwurst

4 oz. (100 g) Cheshire or Cheddar cheese, in one piece

5 tablespoons corn oil

1 onion

1 small apple

2 hard-cooked eggs

½ cup plus 2 tablespoons ketchup

1 tablespoon wine vinegar

Salt

Pinch of sugar

1 teaspoon mild Hungarian paprika

White or black pepper

1 bunch chives

Preheat electric broiler or oven broiling unit.
Make a lengthwise cut down each sausage, slicing ⅔ of the way through.
Cut cheese into strips. Fill sausages with the cheese and brush with some of oil. Broil until cheese melts (about 10 minutes).
Meanwhile, peel and chop onion. Peel, quarter, core and finely chop apple. Shell the eggs and cut into small dice. Combine remaining oil with ketchup, vinegar, salt, sugar, paprika, and pepper. Stir in chopped ingredients and season to taste. Mince chives and stir in. Serve this sauce on the side.

Crepes Florentine

8 small or plum tomatoes (about 1 lb./450 g total)

Salt and white pepper

5 tablespoons (2 ½ oz./75 g) margarine or butter

2 packages frozen creamed spinach in boiling bags (18 oz./540 g total)

¼ cup pancake mix

1 egg

⅓ cup (80 ml) milk

2 teaspoons vegetable oil

Freshly grated nutmeg

2 parsley sprigs

Preheat electric broiler or oven broiling unit.
Rinse and dry tomatoes; score a cross at the top. Season with salt and pepper. Top with 1 tablespoon margarine, cut into tiny bits. Broil for 10 minutes.
Meanwhile, heat spinach according to package directions.
Combine pancake mix, egg, milk, and oil in bowl and whisk to form smooth batter. Melt remaining margarine in 2 skillets. Two at a time, cook 4 crepes about 7 inches (18 cm) in diameter.
Season spinach with salt, if desired, and with nutmeg. Fold crepes around spinach, and arrange on warmed plates. Garnish with broiled tomatoes and a little parsley.

Variations

Shrimp Crepes   Thoroughly drain 1 can (8 oz./ 175 g) mushrooms and 1 can (8 oz./175 g) tiny peas. Sauté with 4 ounces (100 g) diced bacon (strongly smoked variety) over moderate heat. Stir in 7 ounces (200 g) fresh or canned shrimp, heat, and season the mixture. Stir in ¼ cup sour cream and fill crepes with the mixture.

Asparagus Crepes   Heat 10 ounces (300 g) canned asparagus spears (preferably imported white variety) in their canning liquid, drain, and divide among crepes. Melt 2 tablespoons herbed butter (made by creaming butter with premixed *fines herbes* or any preferred herb combination) and drizzle some over each crepe. Top with 1 slice boiled ham apiece and roll up crepes. Sprinkle each with 1 tablespoon grated cheese and serve.

Menu Suggestion

Begin with chicken broth, simmered 5 minutes with ½ leak cut into rings and served with 1 egg yolk per bowl. For dessert, offer vanilla pudding with wafers.

Crepes Florentine are filled with spinach.   ▷

25-Minute Recipes

Given 25 minutes, you can prepare a meal that betrays not the slightest hint of hurry-up. Consider a rustic one-dish dinner like Grilled Sausage with Sauerkraut and Pureed Peas; chicken cutlets in a suave sour cream sauce; beef filet steaks in rich, bacon-scented tomato sauce; pork curry with almonds and fruit. There's even a quick paella!

Grilled Sausages with Sauerkraut and Pureed Peas

20 oz. (570 g) sauerkraut

5 juniper berries

8 sausages of a type suitable for grilling

1 tablespoon vegetable oil

3 cups (750 ml) water

1 package (10 oz./300 g) frozen peas, thawed and pureed in blender

2 slices streaky bacon

2 tomatoes

Parsley

Salt and white pepper

Preheat electric broiler or oven broiling unit.

Place sauerkraut in saucepan and add juniper berries. Heat according to package directions.

Pour boiling water over sausages; wipe dry and brush with oil. Arrange sausages on broiling rack.

Broil about 10 minutes, turning frequently. Meanwhile, bring water to boil in saucepan. Whisk in pureed peas and heat through. Transfer to warmed serving dish. Dice bacon and fry over high heat. Distribute over pea puree.

Arrange sausages on a wooden board. Quarter the tomatoes. Garnish sausages with quartered tomatoes and parsley. Season sauerkraut to taste with salt and pepper and serve.

◁ Grilled Sausages with Sauerkraut and Pureed Peas will please anyone who likes hearty, robust food.   45

25-Minute Recipes

Menu Suggestion
Serve mustard with the sausages and beer or mineral water as a thirst-quencher.

Cottage Cheese Soufflé with Tomato Sauce

1 lb. (450 g) cottage cheese

½ cup (125 ml) milk

2 tablespoons cornstarch

2 eggs

2 slices streaky bacon

4 oz. (125 g) boiled ham

Seasoned salt or pepper

1 teaspoon margarine for baking dish

2 tablespoons breadcrumbs

2 tablespoons (1 oz./30 g) butter

1 cup (240 ml) canned or prepared tomato sauce

Adjust rack to center of oven and preheat oven to 425°F (225°C).

Beat cheese with milk and cornstarch until creamy. Separate eggs. Beat yolks into cheese.

Finely dice bacon and ham. Fold into the cheese mixture and season to taste with all-purpose seasoning. Beat egg whites very stiff and fold into cheese mixture.

Grease 4 small soufflé dishes or 1 large, shallow soufflé dish with margarine. Pour in cheese mixture. Sprinkle with breadcrumbs, then dot with butter.

Bake soufflé(s) for 20 minutes.

Meanwhile, heat tomato sauce. Serve sauce with soufflé.

Menu Suggestion
Begin with beef or veal consommé enriched with mushrooms and cream. With the soufflé, serve a big salad of lettuce or mixed vegetables (make it while the soufflé is in the oven). For dessert, have raspberry pudding or canned peach halves with a little lightly whipped cream.

Calves' Liver with Orange Sauce

1 medium orange

4 slices calves' liver (6 oz./180 g each)

2 tablespoons prepared mustard

3 tablespoons all-purpose flour

¼ cup (60 ml) vegetable oil

Salt

Juice of 3 oranges

1 tablespoon (½ oz./15 g) butter

2 tablespoons orange liqueur

Peel orange and cut into slices.

Spread liver with mustard and toss in flour.

Heat oil in skillet. Sauté liver slices over moderate heat for 3 minutes on each side. Sprinkle with salt; arrange on warmed platter.

Briefly toss orange slices in pan drippings. Arrange over liver slices.

Bring orange juice to boil with the pan juices, scraping up browned bits. Whisk in butter and simmer about 5 minutes to reduce. Pour in orange liqueur. Salt lightly and pour sauce over liver.

Menu Suggestion
Serve with fried potatoes (made from preboiled potatoes), cooked at the same time as the liver.

Brussels Sprouts with Ham

1 ¾ lb. (750 g) Brussels sprouts

3 ½ tablespoons (1 ¾ oz./50 g) butter

Salt

Pinch of freshly grated nutmeg

½ cup (125 ml) beef broth

9 oz. (250 g) lean boiled ham

Out of the ordinary but quickly made: Calves' Liver with Orange Sauce. ▷

Trim and wash Brussels sprouts; score a cross in each stem end.

Melt butter in saucepan and sauté sprouts 3 minutes, shaking the pan. Season with salt and nutmeg. Add hot beef broth and cook the Brussels sprouts, covered, until done, 15 to 20 minutes over gentle heat; they should still have some "bite" and not be falling apart.

Cut ham into long, thin strips and combine with Brussels sprouts, using 2 forks to toss.

Variations

Broccoli salsify or parsnips lend themselves to the same treatment. Freshly grated cheese also adds a piquant note.

Time Tip If you use frozen Brussels sprouts, the recipe will of course be even quicker to prepare. But don't forget to take the package out of the freezer a little in advance.

Filet Steaks with French-Style Peas

½ cup (125 ml) water

1 large package (16 oz./450 g) frozen tiny peas

Salt

1 onion

2 tablespoons (1 oz./30 g) margarine or butter

1 tablespoon all-purpose flour

Pinch of sugar

1 head iceberg lettuce

5 chervil sprigs

¼ cup (60 ml) vegetable oil

4 beef filet steaks (5 oz./150 g each)

White pepper

Garden cress, parsley, or other fresh green herbs for garnish

Bring ½ cup (125 ml) water to boil in saucepan. Add peas and salt. Cook until done, 4 to 6 minutes. Drain, reserving liquid.

Peel and dice onion. Melt margarine in saucepan and sauté onion until translucent. Stir in flour and cook to make a roux. Thin to sauce consistency with cooking liquid from peas. Add peas and season to taste with salt and sugar. Keep warm.

Trim and wash lettuce and cut into very thin strips. Mince the washed chervil. Lightly stir both into the peas. Heat very briefly; transfer to warmed serving dish and keep warm.

Heat oil in skillet. Sear steaks on each side for 30 seconds, then continue to sauté another 3 to 4 minutes per side.

Season with salt and white pepper. Arrange on serving platter and garnish with the garden cress, or serve steaks and peas on individual plates and distribute cress over each serving.

Chicken Cutlets in Cream Sauce with Peas and Carrots

1 ¾ lb. (800 g) chicken cutlets

6 tablespoons (6 oz./90 g) margarine or butter

½ cup (125 ml) hot beef broth

1 heaping teaspoon cornstarch

½ cup (125 ml) sour cream

1 tablespoon soy sauce

Salt and white pepper

1 cup (240 ml) water

1 large package (16 oz./450 g) frozen peas and carrots

1 bunch parsley

Melt 4 tablespoons (2 oz./60 g) butter in skillet. Sauté chicken cutlets over moderate heat just until cooked through, turning several times; do not overcook. Arrange on warmed plates or a deep serving platter, and keep warm.

Bring beef broth to the boil in same skillet, scraping up browned bits. Mix cornstarch to a paste with a little cold water and thicken the sauce with it. Stir in sour cream and soy sauce. Season with salt (if necessary) and pepper. Keep warm.

Meanwhile, bring 1 cup (240 ml) salted water to boil in saucepan. Add unthawed peas and carrots and cook for 8 minutes. Pour off cooking liquid. Melt remaining butter over vegetables. Stir in washed and minced parsley, reserving a few sprigs for garnish.

Arrange vegetables on the platter next to cutlets. Garnish with parsley. Pour a little sauce over cutlets; serve the rest in a warmed sauceboat.

Menu Suggestion

Serve with mashed potatoes, enriched with a little butter and nutmeg and sprinkled with parsley.

Rump Steaks with Buttered Asparagus and Tomatoes

4 rump steaks (6 oz./180 g each)

8 oz. (200 g) canned asparagus tips

1 tablespoon (½ oz./15 g) butter

Pinch each of sugar and salt

2 tomatoes

2 tablespoons vegetable oil

Seasoned pepper

Parsley sprigs

Briefly rinse steaks and blot dry with paper towels. With a sharp knife, score fatty edges at scant ½-inch (1-cm) intervals to prevent meat from curling.

Drain asparagus tips in colander, reserving 1 tablespoon canning liquid. Combine reserved liquid, butter, salt, and sugar in saucepan. Add asparagus and warm over low heat.

Rinse, dry and core tomatoes. Cut into slices.

Heat oil in skillet. Rub steaks with seasoned pepper. Sear in the skillet 30 seconds on each side, then continue sautéing another 4 minutes on each side.

Truly a pleasure: crisp, pan-fried Rump Steaks with Buttered Asparagus and Tomatoes.

Season with salt. Arrange on a wooden platter with asparagus tips and tomato slices on top; sprinkle with seasoned pepper. Garnish with parsley.

Menu Suggestion

Serve with a cucumber-lettuce salad and French bread or mashed potatoes enriched with 1 teaspoon butter and flavored with freshly grated nutmeg. For dessert, have a coconut custard pie.

Filet Steaks on Croutons with Tomato Sauce

4 to 5 small tomatoes (1 lb./450 g total)

½ cup (125 ml) water

1 onion

1 slice streaky bacon

5 tablespoons vegetable oil

2 tablespoons all-purpose flour

½ cup (125 ml) hot beef broth

Pinch of thyme

Pinch of sugar

Salt and white pepper

¼ cup (60 ml) heavy cream

4 beef filet steaks (5 oz./150 g each)

1 small head Boston lettuce

1 tablespoon (½ oz./15 g) butter

4 slices firm-textured bread

Quarter 2 tomatoes for garnish. Rinse the rest and chop finely. Cook with the water in saucepan for 10 minutes over high heat.

A one-plate meal to fit any bill: Filet Steaks on Croutons with Tomato Sauce.

Meanwhile, peel and dice onion; dice bacon. Heat 2 tablespoons oil in saucepan. Sauté bacon until translucent; add onion and cook until golden brown. Stir in flour and cook to make a roux. Pour in hot beef broth, stirring. Press tomatoes through a sieve or food mill into the sauce. Season to taste with thyme, sugar, salt, and white pepper. Add cream and keep warm.

Heat remaining oil in skillet. Sear filet steaks for 30 seconds on each side, then continue to sauté 3 to 4 minutes per side. Salt both sides and season with freshly ground white pepper.

Meanwhile, trim and rinse lettuce; cut into strips.

Melt butter in skillet. Sauté bread slices on both sides until golden brown and arrange on 4 warmed plates. Distribute lettuce, steaks, and sauce over bread slices. Garnish with quartered tomatoes.

Extra-Quick Goulash with Peppers

3 small onions

2 red bell peppers

4 small tomatoes

8 oz. (250 g) canned mushrooms

1 ¼ lb. (600 g) beef filet

¼ cup (60 ml) vegetable oil

Salt, black pepper, pinch of sugar

1 tablespoon mild Hungarian paprika

1 tablespoon soy sauce

Peel and dice onions. Quarter and seed peppers; rinse and cut into large strips. Rinse tomatoes and cut into large cubes, trimming away stem ends.

Leave drained mushrooms whole, or cut into halves or slices.

Cut beef filet into ¾-inch (2-cm) cubes.

Heat oil over high heat in heavy saucepan. Brown beef cubes, tossing constantly, for 3 minutes. Add diced onions and sauté with the meat until golden brown. Season with salt and pepper.

Add bell pepper strips with sugar and paprika. Cover and simmer 10 minutes.

Add diced tomatoes and mushrooms and simmer 5 minutes. Add soy sauce, season to taste and serve.

Variation

Eggplant-Leek Goulash Instead of peppers and mushrooms, add 1 small or ½ medium eggplant (about 10 oz./300 g), rinsed and cut into slices without peeling, and 1 medium leek, rinsed and cut into rings. Season this savory combination with garlic.

Menu Suggestion

To accompany this, offer French bread, pasta or rice with minced parsley. For dessert, have cream-filled vanilla cookies or wafers and ice cream.

> **Time Tip** If you have to cope with guests in a hurry, you'll certainly hit the mark with this pepper goulash. For guests who have announced their arrival well ahead of time, you can make the goulash the night before. Refrigerate it until the next day and you need only heat it up briefly.

Chicken Livers with Peppers

1 lb. (450 g) chicken livers

3 tablespoons cornstarch

1 green and 1 red bell pepper

5 tablespoons vegetable oil

3 tablespoons Sherry

Salt and pepper

Rinse livers, blot dry, and cut in half. Toss in cornstarch. Rinse, core, and seed peppers and cut them into strips.

Heat oil in skillet and sauté liver pieces 1 minute, tossing constantly. Add sliced peppers and sauté with the liver 1 minute, tossing.

Pour in Sherry, reduce heat, and cook at a bare simmer 3 to 5 minutes. Season with salt and pepper.

Menu Suggestion

Serve with rice or fettuccine (or other preferred flat noodles) and a green salad. For dessert, have lemon pudding or mousse.

Pork Cutlet with Cauliflower Mornay

1 small head of cauliflower

Salt and white pepper

4 trimmed lean pork cutlets
  (about 1 ½ lb./650 g total)

3 tablespoons all-purpose flour

1 egg

3 heaping tablespoons breadcrumbs

¼ cup (60 ml) vegetable oil

Mornay sauce:

1 onion

2 tablespoons (1 oz./30 g) butter or margarine

1 tablespoon all-purpose flour

½ cup (125 ml) hot beef broth

1 cup (240 ml) milk

Salt and white pepper

Freshly grated nutmeg

2 oz. (50 g) grated Parmesan or Swiss cheese

¼ cup (60 ml) heavy cream

Divide cauliflower into florets. Rinse and place in a small amount of boiling salted water. Cook until tender, about 15 minutes; drain.

Salt and pepper the pork cutlets. Dip first in flour, then beaten egg and breadcrumbs.

Heat oil in large skillet. Sauté cutlets 7 minutes over medium heat on both sides. Arrange sautéed pork on warmed platter.

For Mornay sauce, peel and chop onion. Melt butter or margarine in saucepan and sauté onion until translucent. Add flour and stir until fat is completely absorbed, then pour in broth and bring to boil. Season with salt, white pepper, and nutmeg. Melt the

Pork Cutlet with Cauliflower Mornay is a full-flavored dish.

cheese in the mixture, stirring. Stir in cream and correct the seasoning. Add cauliflower.

Serve cauliflower and cutlets separately, or arrange together on 4 warmed plates.

Menu Suggestion

Start with oxtail or beef soup heated with ¼ cup tiny peas. With the main course, serve mashed potatoes, sprinkled with minced parsley and seasoned with freshly grated nutmeg. For dessert, offer a fruit salad of dark grapes and unpeeled sliced apples, sprinkled with sugar and perfumed with Calvados (or other apple brandy) and lemon juice. Serve with a vanilla custard sauce or chocolate sauce.

Chicken Breasts Indonesia

4 halved and boned chicken breasts (1 lb./450 g total)

2 tablespoons soy sauce

1 tablespoon Sherry

½ cup (125 ml) beef broth

2 teaspoons cornstarch

Salt

2 small leeks

¼ cup (60 ml) vegetable oil

*2 teaspoons sambal oelek or sambal manis
 (spicy Indonesian flavoring sauces)*

4 small tomatoes

Parsley

Rinse chicken, wipe dry and cut into thin slices.

Mix soy sauce and Sherry with beef broth, cornstarch, and a little salt in a bowl. Toss sliced chicken in the mixture.

Trim and rinse leeks and cut into rings. Heat oil in large, deep skillet. Briefly drain chicken, reserving marinade, and sauté in hot oil 3 minutes, stirring. Remove from skillet and keep warm.

All who love Far Asian cuisine will want to try Chicken Breasts Indonesia.

Rapidly sauté leek rings in fat remaining in the skillet. Pour in marinade and braise 5 minutes.

Return chicken to skillet. Season with *sambal oelek* or *sambal manis*. Adjust seasoning. Serve garnished with tomatoes and parsley.

Menu Suggestion

Serve curried rice; put the rice on to cook before you begin with the other preparations. Steam it fluffy, and season with curry powder. For dessert, offer an exotic salad of pineapple, kiwifruit, and fresh figs, flavored with pomegranate juice. Or serve canned lichees.

> **Cooking Tip** For Indonesian recipes you should use the typical Indonesian flavoring agent, *sambal oelek*. If you'd prefer something a bit milder, then use *sambal manis*, a milder condiment. You can buy both in small jars. These spice mixtures will keep for quite a while if stored in the refrigerator.

Pork Curry with Almonds

Rice:

2 cups (450 ml) water

2 bouillon cubes

1 cup (8 oz./225 g) long-grain or converted rice

Meat:

1 large piece of boneless pork tenderloin, about 1 lb. (450 g)

1 onion

1 tablespoon vegetable oil

1 heaping teaspoon curry powder

1 medium apple

2 slices canned pineapple

1 cup (240 ml) water

1 packet curry sauce mix yielding 1 ¼ to 1 ½ cups (300 to 360 ml) or 1 can (10 oz./300 g) curry sauce

or 1 ¼ cups (300 ml) white sauce flavored with curry powder

3 tablespoons heavy cream

¼ cup (about 1 oz./30 g) sliced almonds

Oil for ramekins

Bring water to boil and dissolve the bouillon cubes. Add rice and bring to boil. Cover and cook until tender, at least 15 minutes.

Meanwhile, rinse and dry pork tenderloin and cut into thick slices. Peel and chop onion.

Heat oil in deep skillet. Briefly cook curry powder in the oil; add meat and sauté rapidly.

Peel, quarter, and core the apple; cut into dice. Dice pineapple slices. Add both to the meat and simmer 10 minutes.

Add water and bring mixture to boil. Add curry sauce and proceed according to package directions. Stir in cream. In a dry skillet, toast slivered almonds until golden brown.

Oil 4 ramekins or custard cups. Press in the rice and turn out onto 4 plates. Sprinkle with toasted almonds. Adjust seasoning of the curry and spoon out around the rice.

Menu Suggestion

Begin with beef noodle soup. With the main course, serve mango chutney, Italian *mostarda di frutta* (fruit and mustard relish), or other spicy condiments. Ice cream is the perfect dessert — perhaps raspberry.

Quick Paella

1 lb. (450 g) frozen cleaned squid

1 lb. (450 g) long-grain rice

¼ cup (60 ml) vegetable oil

4 chicken thighs (1 lb./450 g)

2 onions

1 garlic clove

2 to 3 cups (450 to 700 ml) hot water

1 cup (240 ml) dry white wine

◄ Pork Curry with Almonds is so good that you'll surely make it over and over again.

Salt and black pepper

Large pinch of saffron

16 fresh mussels

20 black olives

10 rock lobster tails, fresh or frozen and thawed

In the morning, place squid in refrigerator to thaw.

Cut drained squid into pieces. Wash rice in a sieve and allow to drain.

Heat oil in paella pan, wok, or large, deep skillet. Quickly brown chicken thighs in hot oil; remove from pan.

Peel and chop onions and garlic clove; sauté until golden in the same oil. Add rice and sauté briefly. Pour in water and wine, stirring. Season with salt and pepper and cook mixture at a bare simmer.

Meanwhile, scrub mussels under running water and remove beards. Add to rice along with chicken thighs, squid, and olives; cook, covered, 20 minutes over low heat, adding more water as necessary. After 10 minutes, gently stir in rock lobster tails and cook until done.

Variation
Simple Paella Instead of mussels and rock lobster tails, use smoked fish and shrimp.

Anchovy Burgers with Mustard-Pickle Sauce

1 onion

5 rolled anchovy fillets with capers

1 lb. (450 g) ground beef

Seasoned pepper

1 tablespoon barbecue sauce

2 eggs

Salt if needed

¼ cup (2 oz./60 g) butter or margarine

8 large chunks of mustard pickle

6 tablespoons evaporated milk

Peel and finely dice onion. Mince anchovies with capers. Mix to a smooth consistency with chopped beef, seasoned pepper, barbecue sauce, and eggs. Add salt if necessary. Form into 8 burgers.

Melt butter or margarine in skillet and sauté hamburgers 8 minutes on each side. Divide among serving plates.

Dice mustard pickle chunks and sauté in pan drippings. Pour in evaporated milk. Bring to boil, scraping up browned bits. Pour over burgers, and serve.

Cream of Leek Soup

1 cup (240 ml) beef broth

1 lb. (450 g) leeks, cleaned and trimmed

1 package (10 oz./300 g) frozen peas

1 hard-cooked egg

½ bunch parsley

Pinch each of salt and white pepper

1 teaspoon fresh lemon juice

½ cup (125 ml) heavy cream

Combine broth, leeks and peas in saucepan, cover and cook over gentle heat until leeks are tender, about 15 minutes.

Shell the egg and dice finely with egg slicer. Rinse parsley, blot dry, and mince.

Press soup through sieve or food mill. Season with salt, pepper, and lemon juice.

Stir half the cream into the soup; whip remaining cream to stiff peaks.

Pour soup into cups and garnish with dollops of whipped cream. Scatter chopped egg and parsley on top.

Menu Suggestion
As accompaniment, serve sourdough rye bread or freshly baked white bread. For dessert, have fruit cocktail or seasonal fresh fruit.

Light and healthful — Cream of Leek Soup. ▷

Calves' Liver with Asparagus Salad

1 lb. (450 g) fresh or canned asparagus, preferably imported white variety

Juice of ½ lemon

1 tablespoon vinegar

Salt and white pepper

Pinch of sugar

¼ cup (60 ml) vegetable oil

4 slices calves' liver (5 oz./150 g each)

1 teaspoon dried rosemary, crushed to release flavor

4 even-sized slices streaky bacon (about 4 oz./400 g total)

4 bay leaves

1 lb. (450 g) green fettuccine (or other flat noodles), cooked the night before

1 tomato

Drain asparagus. Whisk lemon juice with vinegar, salt, white pepper, and sugar; whisk in oil. Gently fold in asparagus and let it absorb the dressing.

Rub calves' liver with rosemary. Lay bacon slices and bay leaves over the slices of liver, and fasten with toothpicks.

Heat oil and butter in large skillet. Sauté liver slices over medium heat 3 to 4 minutes on each side, starting with the bacon side. Remove from skillet and keep warm. Rapidly heat noodles in fat remaining in the skillet, tossing frequently. Blanch tomatoes in boiling water, peel and cut into slices. Arrange liver, noodles, and tomato slices on 4 plates.

Cooking Tip Always salt liver only after cooking; otherwise it toughens. This dish is more economical if you use beef liver.

From the realm of haute cuisine: Calves' Liver with Asparagus Salad.

Skillet-Fried Potatoes and Sausages

3 cold boiled potatoes (about 1 lb./450 g)

¼ cup (2 oz./60 g) butter or margarine

2 onions

2 leeks

*8 oz. (225 g) mild salami, ham loaf,
   or German Bierschinken, in one chunk*

3 tablespoons beef broth

1 tablespoon white wine

Salt and white pepper

1 bunch parsley

Peel potatoes and cut into cubes. Melt butter or margarine in large skillet. Fry potatoes 10 minutes, tossing from time to time.

Peel and dice onions. Trim and rinse leeks; cut into rings. Dice sausage. Add these ingredients to skillet, toss gently to distribute and sauté until golden brown.

Pour in beef broth and white wine. Season with salt and pepper and simmer another 10 minutes, covered. Wash and mince parsley. Serve the dish from the skillet, garnished with parsley.

Variation
Use 8 ounces (225 g) frankfurters and fold in ¼ cup sour cream at the end.

Menu Suggestion
Begin with raw shredded carrots (about 4 large carrots, 10 oz./300 g total) combined with fresh lemon juice, seasonings, 2 tablespoons vegetable oil, and 1 teaspoon soy sauce. Serve the potatoes with mixed pickles; follow with a compote of pears and cranberries or with Raspberry Cream Custard (see Index).

Made quickly and eaten happily: hearty, homespun Skillet-Fried Potatoes and Sausages.

25-Minute Recipes

Chopped Steaks with Broccoli and Quick Tomato Sauce

1 lb. (450 g) broccoli

Salt and garlic powder

2 tablespoons (1 oz./30 g) butter

*2 oz. streaky bacon
(preferably a strongly smoked variety)*

1 garlic clove

1 bunch parsley

1 lb. (450 g) ground beef

¼ cup breadcrumbs

1 egg

Black pepper

¼ cup (60 ml) olive oil

1 cup (240 ml) canned or prepared tomato sauce

1 tablespoon ketchup

Rinse broccoli under running water. Peel the stems. Cut broccoli into pieces. Cook 15 minutes in tightly covered saucepan in a small amount of boiling salted water. Season with garlic powder. Drain; melt butter over the broccoli.

While broccoli is cooking, finely dice bacon; peel garlic clove and crush it with a little salt. Mince parsley. Work ground beef to a smooth consistency with the bacon, crushed garlic, minced parsley, breadcrumbs, egg, and black pepper.

Heat olive oil in skillet. Shape meat mixture into 8 burgers and sauté on both sides 8 minutes. Meanwhile, heat tomato sauce and add ketchup for extra flavoring. Top burgers with sauce and serve with broccoli.

Variation

Chopped Steaks with Green Peppercorns
Mince 1 tablespoon green peppercorns. Rinse, dry and mince 1 bunch chives. Work these into meat mixture along with the other ingredients, then proceed as above.

Menu Suggestion

Serve with potato salad and sweet pickle spears. Dessert could be a fruit sherbet.

Meat Patties with Fried Potatoes and Vegetables

Fried potatoes:

3 medium-size boiled potatoes, cooked the day before (about 1 lb./450 g)

4 tablespoons (2 oz./60 g) margarine or butter

1 onion

Salt

1 red bell pepper

1 can (8 oz./225 g) green beans

Meat patties:

1 dinner roll

2 small onions

*1 lb. (450 g) mixed ground meat
(combination of beef, pork, and veal)*

Black pepper

2 eggs

2 tablespoons barbecue sauce or chili sauce

¼ cup (2 oz./60 g) margarine or butter

Lettuce leaves and parsley sprigs

Peel potatoes and cut into cubes or slices.
Melt 3 tablespoons (1½ oz./45 g) margarine in skillet and fry potatoes over high heat until brown. Peel and chop onion; add to potatoes. Season with salt and fry until crisp over reduced heat.

Meanwhile, quarter and seed the pepper and cut into strips. Steam in tightly covered saucepan with a little salt for no more than 10 minutes.

25-Minute Recipes

Salt the beans and heat in their canning liquid; drain.

Meanwhile, soak roll in water until soft; squeeze dry and crumble. Peel and finely chop onions. Make a smooth, homogeneous mixture with the roll, ground meat, onions, salt, black pepper, eggs, and barbecue or chili sauce. Adjust the seasoning (mixture should be highly flavored). Form into 8 patties.

Melt margarine in large skillet and sauté patties on each side 5 to 6 minutes.

Combine fried potatoes and vegetables. Serve with the patties on lettuce leaves. Garnish with parsley sprigs.

Menu Suggestion
Accompany with an escarole or tomato salad, followed by chocolate layer cake.

Lamburgers on Buns

1 lb. (450 g) finely ground lamb, from shoulder

1 onion

½ red or green bell pepper

1 thick slice celery root (3 oz./100 g)

1 tablespoon tomato paste

1 tablespoon ketchup

1 teaspoon dried herbes de Provence

½ teaspoon Worcestershire sauce

Salt and white pepper

¼ cup breadcrumbs

1 egg

1 tablespoon all-purpose flour

¼ cup (60 ml) vegetable oil

4 large hamburger buns or rolls, halved crosswise

Sauce:

6 tablespoons hot water

1 tablespoon tomato paste

½ red or green bell pepper

1 tablespoon green peppercorns, drained

Garden cress (or other fresh green herbs) and lettuce for garnish

Place ground lamb in bowl. Peel and chop onion; chop bell pepper. Peel and mince celery root. Add these ingredients to the meat along with tomato paste, ketchup, herb mixture (crushed to bring out the flavors), Worcestershire sauce, salt, pepper, breadcrumbs, and egg. Combine to form a smooth mixture.

Scatter flour on work surface. Knead mixture once more and shape into thick log of the same diameter as the halved buns. Cut the log into 8 even slices.

Heat oil in large skillet. Fry lamburgers on both sides until golden, about 8 minutes. Place on halved buns. Arrange on individual plates or on a serving platter.

For the sauce, deglaze skillet with the hot water. Mince bell pepper and add to skillet with tomato paste and green peppercorns. Cook at a bare simmer 5 minutes, stirring occasionally. Pour over the lamburgers. Garnish with cress and lettuce leaves.

Menu Suggestion
Serve with broiled tomatoes: rinse and dry the tomatoes, score a cross at the top, and season with salt and pepper. Place 1 small bit of butter on each tomato and broil 10 minutes. Creamed spinach goes particularly well with this, too; season with fresh lemon juice and freshly grated nutmeg.

Herb-Stuffed Chopped Steaks

1 lb. (450 g) ground beef

1 teaspoon salt

1 teaspoon white pepper

2 teaspoons mild Hungarian paprika

2 teaspoons unsweetened cocoa powder

2 slices day-old white bread

Herb-Stuffed Chopped Steaks are piquant and juicy. ▷

2 egg yolks

5 tablespoons (2 ½ oz./75 g) herbed butter (cream butter with fines herbes or any preferred combination of minced herbs)

3 tablespoons (1 ½ oz./45 g) shortening for frying

Combine beef thoroughly with salt, pepper, paprika, and cocoa. Smooth surface of mixture and cover with parchment paper. Refrigerate for 10 minutes.

Pour hot water over the bread. Let stand 2 minutes, then squeeze dry.

Work egg yolks and bread into meat mixture. With wet hands, form 8 even-sized balls. Using a teaspoon, press a deep depression into each ball. Cut herbed butter into 8 pieces and press 1 piece into each depression. Reshape the mixture into balls and flatten into patties.

Heat fat in skillet and sauté meat patties over moderate heat until brown, about 5 minutes on each side.

Broiled Chicken with Indian Sauce

Bring home a broiled chicken from your favorite take-out shop; it should not be too brown, since it has to be cooked once more. Or you can broil one the night before and finish the preparations shortly before serving time.

5 tablespoons (2 ½ oz./75 g) margarine or butter

1 broiled chicken (about 2 ½ lb./1 ¼ kg)

1 large onion

1 medium-size tart apple

1 tablespoon all-purpose flour

1 tablespoon curry powder

½ cup (125 ml) hot beef broth

1 cup (240 ml) heavy cream

2 tablespoons flaked coconut

1 bunch parsley

Melt 4 tablespoons (2 oz./60 g) margarine or butter in heavy sauce pan and sauté chicken on all sides over moderate heat for 10 minutes. Keep warm.

Peel and chop onion and sauté until golden brown in same fat. Peel, core, and dice the apple and add it; sauté quickly. Sprinkle with flour and stir until browned. Add curry powder and hot beef broth and bring to boil, stirring. Whip the cream and fold it in. Remove from heat.

Melt remaining 1 tablespoon butter in skillet and sauté coconut until golden. Serve chicken carved or whole. Distribute some of sauce over the chicken; pour the rest into a sauceboat. Sprinkle chicken with coconut and garnish with parsley.

Variation
Broiled Chicken with Fruit   Divide a broiled chicken into serving pieces. Drain 1 can fruit cocktail (1 lb./450 g), reserving juice. Melt 1 tablespoon (½ oz./15 g) butter, and sauté chicken pieces. Add fruit and 1 ½ teaspoons fresh lemon juice. Cover tightly and heat through but do not boil. Scatter 2 tablespoons sliced almonds or chopped pistachios over the chicken; set off the flavor with minced fresh mint leaves.

Menu Suggestion
Serve with banana halves sautéed in butter and fluffy white rice flavored with curry. Add rice to boiling water when the chicken has cooked 5 minutes.

Rummy Custard

4 egg yolks

¼ cup (60 g) sugar

3 tablespoons rum

1 cup (240 ml) heavy cream

¾ oz. (20 g) semisweet chocolate

16 small rich sweet biscuits or shortbread cookies

Beat egg yolks with sugar until light and foamy. Stir in half the rum.

Whip cream very stiff and fold into egg mixture.

Pour custard into bowl and coarsely grate or shave chocolate over it.

Sprinkle cookies with remaining rum and garnish the custard with them.

◄   Made with bananas and flavored with coconut flakes: Broiled Chicken with Indian Sauce.

25-Minute Recipes

Raspberry Cream Custard

1 ½ pints (1 lb./500 g) raspberries

1 cup (240 ml) water

Pinch of salt

6 tablespoons cornstarch

½ cup plus 2 tablespoons (3 ½ oz./100 g)
    sugar, or to taste

1 cup (240 ml) heavy cream

Place raspberries in colander and rinse very briefly under running water. Combine half the berries and the water in saucepan and simmer 5 minutes, then press through a sieve.

Bring raspberry puree to boil in saucepan with salt. Mix cornstarch with a little cold water to form a smooth paste. Stir into raspberry puree, bring to boil, and sweeten to taste with sugar.

Press remaining uncooked raspberries through sieve (keeping 4 for garnish) and combine with cooked, thickened raspberry puree.

Whip cream until stiff. Spoon ¼ cup into pastry bag. Fold remaining cream into custard. Divide among 4 dessert glasses. Garnish with whipped cream rosettes and 1 raspberry each.

Strawberry Dream

2 ¼ pints (1 ½ lb./750 g) strawberries

½ cup plus 2 tablespoons (3 ½ oz./100 g) sugar

2 cups (450 ml) buttermilk

Pinch of salt

¼ cup (1 oz./30 g) cornstarch

Juice and grated zest of 1 lemon

2 eggs

Rinse, drain, and hull strawberries. Leave them whole or cut into halves as you prefer. Combine in a bowl with ¼ cup sugar.

In a saucepan, whisk remaining sugar with buttermilk, salt, cornstarch, lemon juice and zest,

and eggs. Bring to boil over low heat, stirring constantly.

Divide strawberries among 4 dessert goblets, reserving a few for garnish. Add custard. Garnish with reserved strawberries and place goblets in cold water to chill.

Cooking Tip In custards and puddings, the average amount needed is somewhere around ½ cup (125 ml) per serving; a dessert for 4 will thus be made with 2 cups (450 ml) of liquid. With fruit salads, you should figure on at least 4 ounces (125 g) of fruit per serving.

Gooseberry-Banana Dessert

1 jar or can (about 1 lb./450 g) gooseberries

6 tablespoons cornstarch

5 tablespoons sugar, or to taste

Pinch of salt

1 teaspoon vanilla extract, or 2 teaspoons
    (1 packet) vanilla sugar

4 bananas

1 carton (8 oz./225 g) plain yogurt

1 tablespoon fresh lemon juice

Drain gooseberries. Pour juice into measuring cup and add enough water to make 2 cups (450 ml). Combine cornstarch and a little of the juice mixture and stir until smooth. Bring remaining juice to boil in saucepan with 2 tablespoons sugar, salt, and vanilla. Add dissolved cornstarch and bring to boil, stirring. Place in cold water bath to cool.

Peel 2 bananas and cut into slices. Combine with gooseberries and divide among dessert glasses. Pour custard over the fruit and allow to cool thoroughly.

Before serving, puree remaining bananas, combine with yogurt and lemon juice and sweeten to taste with remaining sugar. Pour over the dessert.

Choose from Raspberry Cream Custard (foreground), Strawberry Dream (center),
or Gooseberry-Banana Dessert (rear). ▷

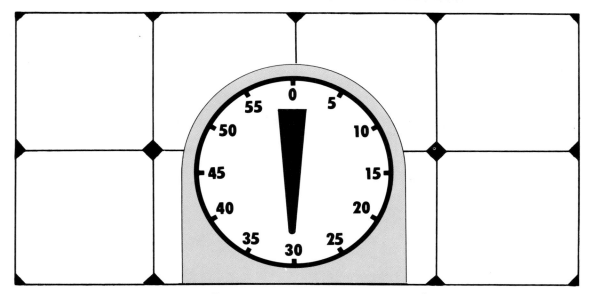

30-Minute Recipes

Turn to this chapter when you have the time, and inclination to spend just a few minutes longer in the kitchen. You will find recipes that are perfect for more leisurely weekend meals, perhaps even for entertaining: herbed Umbrian pork cutlets with tomatoes, and mushrooms, individual pizzas, an unusual Chinese salad made with rice and cellophane noodles. There are several tempting desserts to choose from as well.

Endive Appetizer

2 large Belgian endives

1 tablespoon fresh lemon juice

1 seedless mandarin orange

2 beefsteak tomatoes

4 to 5 stuffed olives

Dressing:

2 tablespoons fresh lemon juice

Pinch of salt

Freshly ground black pepper

2 tablespoons vegetable oil

Wash and trim endive. Halve lengthwise. With a wedge-shaped cut, core out the bitter stalk at the stem end. Brush cut surfaces of endive with lemon juice.

Peel mandarin orange, divide it into segments and carefully remove white membranes. Score a shallow cross on underside of tomatoes and immerse in boiling water for 2 minutes. Skin and quarter tomatoes, remove seeds, and dice the flesh. Cut olives into thin slices. Lightly combine orange sections, diced tomatoes, and olive slices in a bowl.

For the dressing, whisk lemon juice thoroughly with salt, pepper, and oil. Toss salad ingredients with dressing and spoon mixture into the endive halves.

Variation

Endive salad with Apples   Prepare endive as described above. Whisk 2 tablespoons fresh lemon juice with a pinch each of salt and sugar and 2 tablespoons vegetable oil. Wash 1 tart green apple and cut it into eighths without peeling. Remove core and cut into thin slices. Add apple to the dressing at once to keep it from turning brown. Wash and dry 4 ounces (100 g) dark grapes; halve and remove seeds. Coarsely chop 10 walnut meats; crumble 3 ounces (75 g) Roquefort cheese. Add all these ingredients to the sliced apples, combine lightly, and spoon into endive halves.

Menu Suggestion

Accompany with toast or French bread and butter.

◁   Endive Appetizer is especially rich in vitamins.

Chicken Breasts with Summer Vegetables

4 chicken breasts (about 1 lb./450 g)

Salt and white pepper

1 teaspoon curry powder

6 tablespoons (3 oz./90g) margarine or butter

2 packages (10 oz./300 g each) frozen mixed vegetables

1 tablespoon each minced fresh dill and parsley

Skin the chicken breasts. Rub with salt, white pepper, and curry powder.

Melt margarine in deep skillet and brown chicken on all sides for 10 minutes. Add unthawed vegetables. Pour in a little water. Cover tightly and simmer 15 minutes. Stir in dill and parsley.

Menu Suggestion
Begin with Manhattan clam chowder. With the chicken, serve French fries or mashed potatoes. For dessert, offer cherry–vanilla ice cream, fresh fruit, or slices of Zucchini bread.

Veal Cutlets with Potato Croquettes

3 onions

1 large or 2 medium tomatoes (8 oz./225 g)

1 can (8 oz./225 g) green beans

1 can (8 oz./225 g) mushrooms

6 tablespoons (3 oz./90 g) margarine or butter

Salt and black pepper

6 cups (1 ½ L) vegetable oil

4 veal cutlets (about 5 oz./150 g each)

1 package (10 oz./300 g) frozen potato croquettes

Garden cress or other greens for garnish

Peel and slice onions. Pour boiling water over the tomato, peel and chop finely. Drain beans and mushrooms.

Melt 2 tablespoons (1 oz./30 g) margarine in saucepan and sauté 1 sliced onion until golden brown. Add tomato and simmer 5 minutes. Heat beans and mushrooms in tomato mixture. Season with salt and black pepper.

Meanwhile, heat oil to 375°F (180°C) in deep saucepan or electric deep-fryer.

At the same time, melt remaining margarine in skillet. Salt and pepper the veal cutlets and sauté in hot fat 4 minutes on each side, browning remaining sliced onions along with them. Add 3 tablespoons water and cook until onions are soft.

Deep-fry potato croquettes according to package directions. Drain and transfer to serving bowl.

Serve veal cutlets with vegetables on a deep platter. Garnish with garden cress or other greens.

Variation
Veal Cutlets with Mixed Vegetables   Instead of tomatoes, green beans, and mushrooms, cook 2 10-ounce (300 g) packages frozen mixed vegetables (preferably a pre-seasoned combination including sweet peppers, onions, zucchini, and tomatoes) according to package directions. Add sautéed sliced onions.

Tomatoes and Eggplant Mediterranean

8 tomatoes

2 to 3 medium eggplants

1 bunch parsley

3 stalks fresh basil

½ teaspoon salt

2 to 3 tablespoons water

1 garlic clove

White pepper

1 teaspoon all-purpose flour

1 carton (8 oz./225 g) plain yogurt

◄   Chicken Breasts with Summer Vegetables: another offering for those with weight problems.

Score stem ends of tomatoes with a sharp knife and blanch in boiling water 2 minutes. Peel and cut into chunks, trimming away stem end. Wash eggplants and trim stem ends. Peel and cut into even-sized cubes. Wash parsley and basil; chop each separately.

Place tomato and eggplant cubes in large saucepan with the salt and water. Cook over gentle heat until eggplant is tender, about 15 minutes. Force garlic through a garlic press into the vegetables. Add basil and season with white pepper.

Mix the flour with the yogurt, add to the vegetables, and let the mixture boil up a few times. Finally, scatter the parsley over the vegetables.

Umbrian Pork Cutlets

½ bay leaf

½ teaspoon dried rosemary

½ teaspoon dried basil

¼ cup (60 ml) vegetable oil

4 slices (5 oz./150 g each) trimmed boneless pork loin

2 garlic cloves

4 large tomatoes

1 can (8 oz./285 g) mushrooms

Pinch each of salt and black pepper

½ cup (125 ml) white wine

3 to 4 tablespoons grated Parmesan cheese

Crumble bay leaf into small pieces between your fingers. Whisk thoroughly in a small bowl with rosemary, basil, and 2 tablespoons oil. Coat pork cutlets with this mixture and stack on top of each other.

Peel garlic cloves and cut in half lengthwise. Core out stem end of tomatoes and score a shallow cross in the top. Immerse in boiling water for 2 minutes; (peel) and dice coarsely. Drain mushrooms and quarter if large. Heat remaining oil in large skillet and brown garlic cloves; discard them.

Arrange cutlets in the skillet and sauté in hot oil 4 minutes on each side over medium heat. Season with salt and pepper. Pour in white wine and bring to boil. Remove cutlets from skillet and keep warm on a serving platter.

Add diced tomatoes and mushrooms to sauce and let mixture simmer 5 minutes over medium heat. Season to taste with salt and pepper. Pour sauce over the cutlets and sprinkle with Parmesan cheese.

Menu Suggestion

Freshly baked white bread or spaghetti and green salad are good accompaniments. For dessert, serve a maple-walnut torte.

> **Time Tip** Don't sacrifice taste to save what amounts to only a little extra time. Always buy Parmesan cheese by the piece, and grate it freshly just before using it.

Bean Soup and Cheese Snacks

1 large can (16 oz./450 g) hearty bean soup, preferably imported (available in specialty stores)

½ teaspoon dried marjoram, crushed to release flavor

1 tablespoon mild Hungarian paprika

8 lettuce leaves

4 radishes

4 cornichons (small sour gherkins)

4 slices dark whole-grain bread

7 tablespoons (3 ½ oz./100 g) butter

4 slices Gouda cheese, preferably medium-aged (each slice about 3 oz./100 g and ⅜ in./1 cm thick)

½ cup (125 ml) white wine

½ to ¾ cup (100 g) prepared breadcrumb coating mixture

Umbrian Pork Cutlets are imported from the Italian province. ▷

30-Minute Recipes

Prepare bean soup according to directions on can. Season with marjoram and paprika.

Wash lettuce and drain thoroughly. Trim, wash, and dry radishes. Cut cornichons into fan shapes.

Spread slices of bread with 1 tablespoon butter each. Arrange lettuce leaves over bread slices.

Dip cheese slices, one after another, first into white wine, then breading mixture; repeat.

Melt remaining butter in large skillet and quickly fry cheese slices on both sides until golden brown. Cut each in half diagonally. Place on bread slices. Garnish with 1 radish and 1 cornichon fan each. Serve hot, with the hot soup.

Menu Suggestion
Begin with a crabmeat or chicken salad. For dessert, have chocolate pudding or angel food cake.

> **Time Tip** You can give ready-made or canned soup that extra something by adding herbs — for example, parsley, chives, cress, or dill.

Cheeseburgers with Green Peppercorns

4 slices firm-textured bread

2 tablespoons (1 oz./30 g) butter or margarine

1 ½ tablespoons green peppercorns, drained

8 ounces (225 g) ground lean beef sirloin, or a mixture of ground beef, pork, and veal

¼ cup (60 ml) evaporated milk

Salt

Seasoned pepper

4 slices American or Cheddar cheese

1 tomato

Garden cress or other greens for garnish

Preheat electric broiler or oven broiling unit.

Toast bread slices under the broiler on one side. Cool. Spread with butter or margarine.

Meanwhile, crush green peppercorns. Combine ground meat with green peppercorns and evaporated milk. Season with salt and seasoned pepper. Distribute mixture over the bread slices and broil 15 minutes.

Cut packaged cheese slices into strips. Arrange them lattice-fashion over the toasted sandwiches. Broil until cheese melts. Garnish with tomato slices and cress or other greens.

Menu Suggestion
Begin with a shredded raw carrot salad seasoned with fresh lemon juice and a pinch each of sugar, salt, and pepper, mixed with 2 tablespoons chopped hazelnuts. For dessert, serve an apple tart.

Tomato Soup with Quick Cutlets

2 packages (10 oz./300 g each) stuffed veal or chicken cutlets

6 tablespoons (3 oz./90 g) margarine or butter

2 onions

1 lb. (450 g) canned peeled tomatoes

2 tablespoons instant beef broth

2 tablespoons all-purpose flour

1 tablespoon tomato paste

Salt and white pepper

Pinch of sugar

3 drops hot pepper sauce

½ cup (125 ml) heavy cream

1 egg yolk

1 bunch chives

1 tomato

Parsley

Let stuffed cutlets thaw 10 to 15 minutes if frozen.

Meanwhile, melt 2 tablespoons (1 oz./30 g) margarine in saucepan. Peel and dice onions;

sauté until golden brown. Add tomatoes and instant broth (with a little hot water if necessary). Simmer 5 minutes and force through sieve or food mill. Return to boil. Mix flour with a little water to form a smooth paste. Whisk into tomato soup to thicken. Season with tomato paste, salt, pepper, sugar, and hot pepper sauce.

Whisk cream together with egg yolk. Stir into hot soup and heat but do not boil. Wash and mince chives; stir into soup.

Melt remaining margarine in large skillet. Fry cutlets until golden brown, 6 to 8 minutes. Arrange on warmed platter and garnish with tomato and parsley. Serve tomato soup first, then the cutlets.

Menu Suggestion

Have a green salad with the best greens of the season — head lettuce, escarole, mâche, iceberg lettuce, or endive. And perhaps Chinese cabbage; you need only trim it and cut it into bite-sized pieces.

Cooking Tip Be sure to use hot pepper sauce carefully in seasoning; it is so potent that it should be used only drop by drop. It's useful for seasoning soups and sauces, meat, fish, poultry, and egg dishes, as well as hearty vegetable stews.

Pan-Fried Sausages with Raisin Sauerkraut

¼ cup (2 oz./60 g) margarine or butter

2 large onions

1 ¼ lb. (560 g) mild sauerkraut

½ cup (125 ml) light white wine

¾ cup (85 g) raisins

Salt and white pepper

¼ cup (60 ml) vegetable oil

1 pound (450 g) narrow bratwurst or all-beef
   frankfurters

Melt margarine in saucepan. Peel and dice the onions and brown lightly in the fat.

Add sauerkraut to saucepan, fluffing the strands lightly. Bring to simmer. Pour in white wine, cover tightly and simmer 10 minutes. Add raisins and simmer 10 minutes longer. Season finished sauerkraut with salt and white pepper.

Meanwhile, heat oil in skillet. Add sausages and cook until crisply browned on all sides, about 10 minutes.

Variation

Dutch-Style Sauerkraut   Quickly sauté onions in fat. Add sauerkraut. Stir in white wine, 1 bouillon cube, and 2 cored and sliced apples and braise 5 minutes. Thicken cooking liquid with a *beurre manié*: knead together 1 tablespoon softened butter and 1 tablespoon all-purpose flour, drop by bits into the sauerkraut, and allow to boil 2 minutes, stirring.

Menu Suggestion

Begin with pickled herring cocktail. With the main dish, serve mashed potatoes or coarse country-style sourdough rye bread. For dessert, divide 4 peeled and diced oranges among 4 dessert glasses; spoon lemon pudding on top.

Quick Chili Con Carne

(For 3 people)

1 large can (15 oz./425 g) good-quality chili
   (without beans)

2 tablespoons (1 oz./30 g) margarine or butter

2 onions

1 garlic clove

2 tablespoons tomato paste

Salt

1 teaspoon dried oregano

Large pinch of chili powder

1 can (15 oz./425 g) kidney beans

◄   Pan-Fried Sausages with Raisin Sauerkraut are a pleasure not to be missed.

Place chili in large saucepan and bring to simmer. Cover and simmer for 10 minutes.

Melt margarine in another saucepan. Peel and slice onions; chop garlic. Add to hot margarine with tomato paste and sauté until onion is translucent.

Add to chili along with seasonings and kidney beans. Heat for 5 minutes and adjust seasonings (flavor should be robust).

Menu Suggestion

Offer a mixed vegetable salad along with corn bread squares. For dessert, a flan or fruit cocktail.

Serbian-Style Codfish Fillets

(For 2 people)

2 onions

2 tablespoons (1 oz./30g) margarine or butter

½ cup (125 ml) white wine

1 package (16 oz./450 g) frozen mixed vegetables (preferably including leeks, carrots, bell peppers, corn, mushrooms)

Salt and black pepper

1 garlic clove

1 package (16 oz./450 g) frozen codfish fillets (unbreaded)

1 tablespoon mild Hungarian paprika

Garlic powder

Pinch of sugar

1 tablespoon minced fresh parsley

Peel onions and cut into rings. Melt margarine in heavy large saucepan and quickly sauté onions until golden brown.

Add ¼ cup white wine and frozen mixed vegetables. Season with salt and pepper. Peel garlic clove, crush with a little salt, and add to saucepan. Simmer, covered, for 5 minutes.

Meanwhile, sprinkle codfish fillets with remaining wine (the wine's acids will help firm them). Season with salt and pepper and sprinkle with paprika and garlic powder. Lay fillets on top of vegetables and cook 20 minutes at a bare simmer over low heat.

Carefully lift fish fillets from the pan with slotted spoon or skimmer. Add sugar to vegetables and adjust seasoning. Stir in parsley. Transfer vegetables to warmed serving dish and arrange codfish fillets on top. Sprinkle with a little more paprika if desired.

Menu Suggestion

Begin with a simple green salad with creamy cucumber dressing. With the codfish fillets, serve fluffy white rice; mix the rice with a small amount of canned diced pimientos. For dessert, have coffeecake or sliced fresh pineapple.

Ocean Perch Fillets with Herb Sauce

4 wide, thin ocean perch fillets (7 oz./200 g each)

Juice of 1 lemon

Salt

3 tablespoons (1 ½ oz./45 g) butter or margarine

1 cup (240 ml) dry white wine

½ bunch parsley

4 tarragon sprigs

4 chervil sprigs

2 tablespoons all-purpose flour

White pepper

2 teaspoons Worcestershire sauce

2 tablespoons (1 oz./30 g) herbed butter (cream butter with fines herbes or any preferred combination of minced herbs)

Parsley sprigs and lemon slices for garnish

Adjust rack to center of oven and preheat oven to 400°F (200°C).

Briefly rinse fish fillets under cold water. Drain on paper towels. Arrange on platter and sprinkle with lemon juice. Season with salt.

Grease large baking dish with a little of the butter or margarine. Lay fish fillets in it and pour white wine over them. Dot with 1 tablespoon butter. Bake until fish is just opaque, not more than 12 minutes.

Meanwhile, wash and mince herbs.

Arrange fish fillets on warmed platter. Melt remaining butter or margarine in skillet. Stir in flour and cook to make a roux. Stir in the fish cooking juices and cook 2 minutes. Gently stir in herbs. Season sauce to taste with salt, white pepper, and Worcestershire sauce. Whisk in herbed butter.

Pour herb sauce over fish. Serve the dish garnished with parsley and lemon slices.

Menu Suggestion

Serve a mixed salad, if you have the time to make it; otherwise take-out coleslaw or marinated vegetables. Also offer mashed potatoes or canned new potatoes gently fried in a little fat.

Turkey Cutlets with Pineapple

4 turkey cutlets (5 oz./150 g each)

3 tablespoons (1 ½ oz./45 g) butter or margarine

Salt and white pepper

4 slices canned pineapple

1 tablespoon white rum

Large pinch of curry powder

Blot turkey dry on paper towels.

Melt 2 tablespoons (1 oz./30 g) butter in skillet and sauté turkey on both sides 2 to 3 minutes. Salt, pepper, and keep warm.

Drain pineapple slices. Melt remaining butter in same skillet and sauté pineapple until golden. Drizzle with rum and season with curry powder.

Arrange turkey cutlets over pineapple slices on warmed platter. Drizzle with pan juices and serve.

Menu Suggestion

Accompany with brown rice and green beans. For dessert, have marble cheesecake.

Pork in Sweet and Sour Sauce

1 pound (450 g) pork butt

1 tablespoon dry Sherry

2 tablespoons soy sauce

Pinch each of salt and black pepper

8 oz. (225 g) canned pineapple chunks, drained

8 oz. (225 g) canned mandarin orange segments, drained

3 tablespoons cornstarch

¼ cup (60 ml) vegetable oil

½ cup (125 ml) hot beef broth

2 tablespoons vinegar

2 tablespoons sugar

Cut pork into ¾-in. (2-cm) cubes.

Whisk Sherry with 1 tablespoon soy sauce, salt, and pepper in a bowl large enough to hold meat. Place meat cubes in marinade and toss thoroughly; cover and let stand 5 minutes to absorb marinade.

Pour pineapple chunks and mandarin orange segments into colander and drain well.

Sprinkle cornstarch over marinated meat cubes.

Heat oil in heavy saucepan and brown meat 5 minutes over high heat, stirring.

Deglaze with beef broth; stir in vinegar and sugar. Add drained pineapple chunks and mandarin orange segments and bring to boil.

Season to taste with salt and remaining soy sauce.

Menu Suggestion

Serve with fluffy white or brown rice, cellophane noodles cooked according to package directions, or egg noodles, either sautéed in oil or tossed in butter. For dessert, have coconut custard pie.

Perfectly harmonized in both color and flavor: Pork in Sweet and Sour Sauce. ▷

Toasted Cheese Sandwiches with Fried Eggs

4 slices firm-textured white bread

3 tablespoons (1 ½ oz./45 g) butter or margarine

1 cup (240 ml) dry white wine

7 ounces (200 g) grated Gruyère or Swiss Emmenthal cheese

1 garlic clove

Salt

5 eggs

White pepper

¼ cup (60 g) green peppercorns, drained

Spread slices of bread with 1 tablespoon (½ oz./15 g) softened butter or margarine. Arrange buttered side down in large, shallow baking dish. Sprinkle bread with a little white wine.

Adjust rack to upper third of oven and preheat oven to 350°F (175°C).

Combine remaining wine with grated cheese. Peel garlic clove, and crush with a little salt. Stir into cheese mixture with 1 egg. Season mixture to taste with salt and freshly ground white pepper. Gently stir in green peppercorns.

Distribute cheese mixture over bread slices. Bake 7 to 8 minutes.

Meanwhile, melt remaining butter or margarine in large skillet and fry remaining 4 eggs sunny side up.

Cut toasted cheese sandwiches in half and arrange on warmed plates. Slide 1 egg onto each and serve at once.

Variation

Cheese and Red Pepper Sandwiches   For this, use 7 ounces (200 g) grated medium-aged Gouda cheese; instead of green peppercorns, use 1 very finely minced red bell pepper or a few tablespoons of canned sliced pimiento.

Menu Suggestion

Begin with a simple vegetable soup. With the sandwiches, serve a bell pepper salad or a meat and vegetable salad. Alternatively, slice 2 medium tomatoes and 1 cucumber and toss with a dressing of vinegar, salt, garlic powder, minced chives, and olive or vegetable oil; add a bit of chopped onion if you wish. For dessert, offer a wine aspic with vanilla custard sauce.

Pizza with Vegetables

½ package (17 ¼ oz./489 g) frozen puff pastry

1 tablespoon all-purpose flour

Topping:

8 oz. (225 g) tomatoes (about 2 medium or 3 or 4 small tomatoes)

1 green bell pepper

8 oz. (225 g) Chinese cabbage or leeks

1 small jar (3 oz./85 g) capers

5 anchovy fillets packed in oil

Salt and black pepper

1 teaspoon dried oregano

¼ cup (60 ml) olive oil

8 oz. (225 g) mozzarella (or Edam) cheese, in one side

Parsley, garden cress, or other fresh green herbs

In the morning, place 1 wrapped sheet of puff pastry in refrigerator to thaw.

Working on a surface dusted with flour, cut five 4 ½-in. (12-cm) rounds from puff pastry sheet. Rinse 5 tartlet tins with cold water and line with pastry rounds.

Adjust rack to center of oven and preheat oven to 500°F (250°C).

Rinse and dry tomatoes; cut into thick slices. Rinse, core, and seed green pepper; cut into thin rings. Trim and rinse Chinese cabbage or leeks, drain, and cut up coarsely. Drain the capers.

A meal for funlovers: Pizza with Vegetables.   ▶

Top tartlets with 1 anchovy fillet apiece. Over this, distribute prepared vegetables and some oil from the anchovies. Sprinkle with salt, black pepper, and oregano; drizzle with olive oil.

Cut mozzarella or Edam cheese into short, thick slices. Distribute over the topping; scatter with parsley.

Bake pizzas 15 minutes. Serve hot.

Menu Suggestion

With the pizza, serve a big bowl of green salad; for dessert, have spumoni ice cream or a frozen biscuit tortoni.

Chinese Rice and Noodle Salad

½ cup (115 g) long-grain rice

1 ounce (25 g) cellophane noodles

1 cup (7 oz./200 g) leftover roast meat

⅓ cup (2 oz./50 g) unsalted peanuts

8 oz. (300 g) canned mandarin orange segments

1 head Boston lettuce

6 tablespoons soy sauce

1 tablespoon sugar

Pinch each of salt, white pepper, and ground ginger

2 tablespoons vegetable oil

Bring a generous amount of salted water to boil, scatter in the rice, and cook until tender, 15 minutes. Pour cooked rice into colander and drain.

Pour boiling water over cellophane noodles and soak 5 minutes. Cut up coarsely and let cool.

Dice leftover meat and combine in bowl with peanuts and mandarin oranges (with canning liquid).

Pull apart lettuce leaves, wash, drain (or spin in salad spinner), and tear into large pieces. Line a platter with the lettuce.

Chinese Rice and Noodle Salad can be quickly prepared from leftovers.

Whisk soy sauce thoroughly with sugar, salt, white pepper, ginger, and oil in small bowl.

Lightly toss all prepared salad ingredients in large bowl.

Mound salad over lettuce leaves. Pour dressing on top and blend into salad with 2 forks.

Variation

Instead of leftover roast meat, use leftovers from poached or broiled chicken. Boiled ham, cut into small cubes, is equally good in this salad.

Cold Cucumber Soup with Walnuts

3 cucumbers

Salt

2 garlic cloves

1 scant cup (3 ½ oz./100 g) shelled walnuts

3 tablespoons vegetable oil

1 quart (950 ml) buttermilk

½ cup (125 ml) milk

½ cup (125 ml) sour cream

Pinch each of salt and freshly ground pepper

½ teaspoon fresh lemon juice

1 bunch dill

Peel cucumbers and halve lengthwise. Scrape out seeds with a teaspoon. Finely shred cucumbers, then toss with a little salt, cover, and refrigerate.

Force garlic cloves through a garlic press, or peel and coarsely chop them, sprinkle with a little salt and crush with a fork.

Reserve a few walnut meats for decoration; finely grind the rest.

Cold Cucumber Soup with Walnuts — refreshing and piquant.

Beat oil, buttermilk, milk, and sour cream with electric mixer at high speed until smooth.

Stir in garlic, ground nuts, and shredded cucumbers. Season soup with salt, pepper, and lemon juice. Refrigerate.

Rinse dill, blot dry and mince. Garnish cucumber soup with a sprinkling of dill and reserved walnut meats. Serve with fresh French bread.

Potato Pancakes with Ham and Cheese

1 package (6 oz./170 g) potato pancake mix

2 cups (450 ml) cold water

2 large tomatoes

1 onion

6 tablespoons vegetable oil

2 large slices (scant ¼ in./ ½ cm thick) lean boiled ham

8 slices American or Cheddar cheese

1 tablespoon minced chives

In mixing bowl, beat potato pancake mix with water. Let stand 10 minutes to absorb liquid.

Rinse, dry the tomatoes and cut into 4 slices each. Peel and evenly dice onions.

Preheat electric broiler or oven broiling unit.

Heat oil in large skillet. Fry potato pancakes in 2 batches of 8 small pancakes each.

Cut ham slices into quarters. Place 1 piece of ham and 1 cheese slice apiece on 8 of the pancakes (keep remaining pancakes warm). Run under pre-heated broiler 5 minutes or until cheese melts. Top with remaining potato pancakes. Distribute 1 slice of tomato apiece, the diced onion, and minced chives over pancakes and serve at once.

Variations

Potato Pancakes and Smoked Tongue   Briefly heat thick slices of smoked tongue or blood and tongue sausage in a little butter in skillet. Sandwich between cooked pancakes, and serve.

Potato Pancakes with Fruit and Cottage Cheese
Fry potato pancakes as directed. While they cook, combine 8 ounces (225 g) cottage cheese with a little heavy cream and fruit (for example, fruit cocktail). Sweeten to taste and fill each pancake sandwich with the mixture.

Time Tip In preparing foods from ready-made or partly precooked products, always pay attention to the directions on the package. For example, you must never deep-fry potato pancakes made from a mix: they will sputter fiercely on account of their water content.

French Toast with Tomato-Beef Soup

1 can (19 oz./543 g) tomato soup with vegetables and macaroni

1 large leek

½ bunch parsley

8 oz. (225 g) ground beef

½ cup (100 g) seasoned breadcrumbs

2 eggs

5 tablespoons (2 ½ oz./75 g) margarine or butter

1 cup (240 ml) milk

Salt

4 slices white bread

2 tablespoons sugar

1 teaspoon cinnamon

Place soup in saucepan. Wash and trim leek, cut into thin rings, and add to soup. Mince parsley and add to saucepan. Heat gently.

Mix meat with breadcrumbs. Add ½ lightly beaten egg and blend well. Shape into balls about 1 inch (2 cm) in diameter. Sauté meatballs in 1 table-spoon (½ oz. / 15 g) margarine until crisp and browned on all sides, about 5 minutes. Drain on paper towels, then add to soup.

French Toast is a perfect accompaniment to a hearty Tomato-Beef Soup.   ▷

Meanwhile, whisk milk lightly with remaining 1½ eggs and salt. Add bread and soak 5 minutes.

Melt margarine in large skillet. Sauté lightly drained bread slices on each side until golden brown, about 4 minutes.

Serve French toast after the soup; sprinkle with sugar and cinnamon.

Variation

Carthusian Dumplings These are prepared from day-old rolls, cut in half and crusts removed, softened in the egg-milk mixture, coated with bread-crumbs and browned on all sides in hot margarine for 5 minutes. Eat them with sugar and cinnamon.

Rice Condé

1 can (8 oz./240 g) apricots

2 tablespoons Kirsch

Pinch of salt

1 cup (8 oz./225 g) long-grain rice

2 cups (450 ml) milk

¾ cup (5 oz./100 g) sugar

1 strip lemon zest

½ vanilla bean

1 tablespoon (½ oz./15 g) butter

Place apricots in bowl with half of their canning liquid. Add Kirsch, cover, and let stand for fruit to absorb liquor.

Bring generous amount of salted water to boil. Scatter in rice and cook 5 minutes. Drain in sieve.

Bring milk to boil with sugar, lemon zest, and vanilla bean (slit open to release flavor). Add drained rice and cook at a very gentle simmer for 20 minutes over low heat, stirring occasionally. Remove vanilla bean and lemon zest.

Combine butter with cooked rice and spoon into bowl. Arrange apricots on rice and pour juice over.

Rice Condé is a well-known dessert.

Pork and Rice with Mushrooms

8 oz. (225 g) pork shoulder butt

2 onions

1 garlic clove

1 tablespoon (½ oz./15 g) margarine or butter

1 cup (8 oz./225 g) long-grain rice

3 cups (700 ml) beef broth

Pinch each of salt and white pepper

½ teaspoon dried thyme

6 ounces (175 g) canned mushrooms

1 to 2 teaspoons soy sauce

1 teaspoon minced fresh parsley

Cut meat into thin strips. Peel and finely chop onions and garlic clove.

Melt margarine in skillet large enough to hold all ingredients. Sear strips of meat 2 minutes, turning frequently. Add onions and garlic. Scatter in the rice and sauté with meat for 5 minutes over moderate heat, stirring constantly. Pour in beef broth a little at a time. Season mixture with salt, white pepper, and thyme.

Let the mixture simmer gently 10 minutes over low heat, stirring occasionally.

Drain mushrooms and cut into small pieces. Combine with rice mixture and let all ingredients cook another 5 minutes.

Season to taste with soy sauce and sprinkle with parsley.

Variation

The meat-rice mixture can be further embellished with ½ package (10 oz./300 g) frozen peas. The dish

Not exactly inexpensive, but quite delicious: Pork and Rice with Mushrooms.

is still more appealing when seasoned with 2 teaspoons curry powder.

Menu Suggestion
Begin with tomato juice with freshly minced herbs — or seasoned only with salt and pepper. Accompany with an endive or chicory salad. For dessert, have fresh fruit or a lemon mousse.

Ham and Endive Ragout

1 lb. (450 g) Belgian endive

2 tablespoons (1 oz./30 g) butter

8 oz. (225 g) lean boiled ham or picnic shoulder

8 oz. (225 g) tomatoes
(about 2 medium or 3 or 4 small tomatoes)

Salt and white pepper

2 tablespoons fresh lemon juice

1 tablespoon Worcestershire sauce

2 cups (450 ml) white sauce (any preferred recipe, or use 1 ½ cans (10 ½ oz./300 g each) prepared white sauce

1 egg yolk

2 tablespoons sour cream

½ bunch parsley

Remove any withered leaves from endive. With a wedge-shaped cut, core out root end. Cut endive into 1¼-inch (3-cm) pieces.

Melt butter in saucepan. Braise endive 5 to 8 minutes or until crisp-tender, stirring occasionally.

Meanwhile, cut ham into strips. Rinse and dry tomatoes and cut into eighths. Add to endive and simmer another 5 minutes. Season with salt and white pepper, lemon juice, and Worcestershire sauce.

Prepare white sauce and blend in egg yolk and sour cream. Add sauce to ragout and bring to boil briefly, stirring. Remove from heat. Wash and mince parsley, stir in, and serve.

Variation
Asparagus Ragout with Salami Cut 8 ounces (225 g) mild Bierwurst, ham loaf or soft Italian salami into cubes. Sauté 5 minutes in 2 tablespoons butter with 1 chopped onion. Add tomatoes and — instead of Worcestershire — soy sauce. Prepare and add white sauce. Add 1 pound (450 g) drained canned asparagus and heat through. Season to taste and serve.

Menu Suggestion
Begin with beef noodle soup, sprinkled with cress or other fresh green herbs and piquantly seasoned with 3 drops hot pepper sauce. With the ragout your best bet would be white rice, seasoned with a dusting of paprika; put it on to cook before you begin making the ragout. You can also serve boiled parsley potatoes, if you prefer. For dessert, offer apple pie with whipped cream.

> **Cooking Tip** Any of the suggested ragout versions can be sprinkled with chopped, slivered or sliced almonds or sliced hazelnuts, toasted (with or without fat) in a skillet. Be sure to stir them often, since nuts scorch quickly.

Breton-Style Pork Chops

4 pork chops (5 oz./150 g each)

Salt and black pepper

¼ cup (60 ml) vegetable oil

2 cans (15 oz./425 g each) white beans

1 onion

3 tablespoons (1 ½ oz./45 g) butter

½ cup (125 ml) white wine

2 tablespoons tomato paste

1 garlic clove

1 bunch parsley

◁   Ham and Endive Ragout is just the dish for those who prefer lighter fare.

Rinse off pork chops and dry with paper towels. Rub with salt and black pepper. Heat oil in skillet. Sear chops on both sides, then sauté until done, 5 minutes per side.

Meanwhile, drain beans in colander, reserving liquid. Heat beans in a saucepan. Peel and chop onion; in another saucepan, sauté in 1 tablespoon hot butter until golden. Pour in ½ cup (125 ml) of bean liquid and simmer 5 minutes to reduce.

Add white wine and tomato paste. Peel garlic clove, crush with a little salt, and add to mixture. Bring to vigorous boil. Press through sieve or food mill.

Wash parsley; let drain on paper towels. Set aside a few sprigs for garnish. Mince the rest and mix into sauce with remaining 2 tablespoons butter.

Arrange the chops on warmed serving plates or platter. Distribute some of the sauce over them, and serve remainder on the side. Garnish with parsley sprigs.

Menu Suggestion

Serve 8 broiled tomatoes as accompaniment. Score a cross in stem end of each tomato, dot with a small amount of butter, and broil 10 minutes while preparing sauce. In addition, potato puffs or a warm potato salad would go well. For dessert, serve a jellyroll with whipped cream.

Pork Cutlets in Cream Sauce

4 slices boneless pork loin (about 5 oz./150 g each)

White pepper

2 tablespoons all-purpose flour

3 oz. (100 g) fresh mushrooms

2 tablespoons vegetable oil

2 tablespoons (1 oz./30 g) butter

Salt

1 cup (240 ml) heavy cream

Rub cutlets with a little pepper and toss in flour. Clean and slice mushrooms.

Heat oil and butter in skillet and sauté cutlets 5 minutes on each side. Salt after sautéing. Transfer to heated platter and keep warm.

Sauté mushroom slices, tossing, in same skillet. Stir in cream and scrape up browned bits from bottom of skillet. Let sauce boil briefly, season to taste with salt and pepper and pour over cutlets.

Menu Suggestion

Serve fluffy white rice and buttered peas, or a green salad and French bread. For dessert, have lemon cake or chocolate pudding.

Bohemian Pork Steaks

4 slices boneless pork shoulder butt (about 6 oz./180 g each)

2 tablespoons prepared mustard

1 tablespoon mild Hungarian paprika

1 tablespoon all-purpose flour

3 oz. (100 g) streaky bacon

4 onions

Pound meat slices well to tenderize. Spread with mustard and sprinkle with paprika. Place flour on shallow plate and lightly coat slices of meat in it.

Finely dice bacon. Peel and slice onions. Render diced bacon in skillet large enough to hold all ingredients. Add onion rings and sauté until browned. Push bacon and onions to one side of skillet.

Add pork to skillet and sauté 4 to 5 minutes on each side over moderate heat. Arrange all ingredients on warmed platter and serve.

Menu Suggestion

Begin with a smoked fish pâté. Serve noodles or fried potatoes and red cabbage with the pork. For dessert, have cheese strudel.

A lusty dish: Bohemian Pork Steaks. ▷

30-Minute Recipes

Cherry Rice Pudding

1 cup (240 ml) milk

½ vanilla bean

2 cups (6 oz./175 g) rice cooked in milk

4 egg whites

6 tablespoons sugar

1 lb. (450 g) canned sour cherries

2 tablespoons (1 oz./30 g) butter or margarine

Preheat oven to 500°F (250°C) or broiler to highest possible temperature.

Heat milk with vanilla bean (slit open to release flavor), add rice, and warm for several minutes over low heat. Remove vanilla bean.

Beat egg whites until stiff. Gradually add sugar and beat until whites stand in glossy peaks.

Drain cherries. Generously coat baking dish with butter or margarine and pour in cherries. Fold beaten egg whites into rice mixture and mound over the cherries. Bake until meringue is lightly browned. Serve warm.

Breaded Calves' Brains

1 ¼ lb. (575 g) calves' brains

2 tablespoons vinegar

2 cups (500 ml) boiling water

Salt and white pepper

2 tablespoons all-purpose flour

1 egg

3 tablespoons breadcrumbs

3 tablespoons (1 ½ oz./45 g) butter or margarine

Carefully rinse calves' brains. Combine vinegar and boiling water and pour over brains. Cover and let stand 10 minutes.

Remove outer membranes and cut brains into slices. Season with salt and pepper. Coat first in flour, then in beaten egg, and finally in breadcrumbs.

Melt butter in skillet and sauté slices on both sides until golden, about 5 minutes.

Menu Suggestion
Serve with chive-flavored scrambled eggs and sliced tomatoes or with buttered peas and parsley potatoes or French bread. For dessert, offer coffee ice cream.

Venetian Calves' Liver

2 onions

1 lb. (450 g) calves' liver

¼ cup (60 ml) olive oil

¼ teaspoon dried sage

Pinch each of salt and black pepper

2 tablespoons wine vinegar

1 tablespoon dry white wine

½ bunch parsley

Peel onions and cut into thin slices. Cut liver into strips about ⅜ inch (1 cm) wide and blot dry with paper towels.

Heat 2 tablespoons oil in skillet and sauté onion slices over gentle heat until translucent, tossing frequently. Add sage and sauté another 2 to 3 minutes or until onions are light brown.

Rapidly heat remaining oil in second skillet and brown liver strips 2 to 3 minutes on all sides, tossing. Add sliced onions and sauté for 1 minute.

Season with salt and pepper and transfer to warmed serving platter.

Deglaze pan drippings with vinegar and wine and pour over liver and onions.

Rinse parsley, blot dry and mince. Scatter over liver before serving.

Menu Suggestion
Serve with spaghetti, tossed with butter and Parmesan cheese and a green salad. For dessert, offer cannoli, rum cake or other Italian pastries.

The exquisite flavor of Venetian Calves' Liver comes from sage. ▷

30-Minute Recipes

Pork Stir-Fry

1 lb. (450 g) boneless pork shoulder

2 onions

6 mushrooms

8 oz. (225 g) celery root, Chinese cabbage or bok choy

1 red and 1 green bell pepper

¾ cup (4 oz./125 g) bean sprouts

1 ½ teaspoons salt

1 teaspoon white pepper

¼ cup (60 ml) vegetable oil

¼ cup (60 ml) soy sauce

Cut meat into thin strips. Peel and slice onions. Clean mushrooms and cut into quarters.

If using celery root, peel and slice as thinly as possible. If using cabbage or bok choy, cut into thin strips.

Halve, core, and seed peppers; rinse and dice finely. Turn bean sprouts into colander, rinse with cold water and drain.

Combine all prepared ingredients in bowl and season with salt and pepper.

Heat oil in wok or skillet. Add meat-vegetable mixture and stir-fry 10 to 15 minutes over moderate heat. Stir in soy sauce before serving.

Menu Suggestion
Serve with fluffy steamed rice or rice noodles. For dessert, offer canned lychees or other Oriental fruit and fortune cookies.

> **Cooking Tip** If you freeze the meat briefly before starting, it will be easier to slice.

Pork Cutlets Orvieto

4 slices boneless pork loin (about 5 oz./100 g each)

Salt and pepper

½ teaspoon each dried oregano, thyme, and rosemary

3 tablespoons (1 ½ oz./45 g) butter

4 slices mild-flavored cheese, each ¼ inch (½ cm) thick

Press cutlets flat with the palm of your hand. Season with salt and pepper.

Combine oregano, thyme, and rosemary in small bowl and rub cutlets with half of the mixture.

Melt butter in skillet and sauté cutlets 5 minutes on each side.

Preheat broiler.

Arrange sautéed cutlets next to each other in broilerproof dish, cover with cheese slices and scatter with remaining herbs. Deglaze pan drippings with a small amount of water and pour around cutlets.

Run cutlets under the broiler until cheese is golden brown.

Menu Suggestion
Offer steamed broccoli and boiled potatoes, or steamed cauliflower and parsley potatoes. For dessert, have baked apples with whipped cream.

Quick Chicken Liver Risotto

1 onion

3 tablespoons olive oil

¾ cup (7 oz./200 g) Italian arborio or other short-grain rice

2 cups (450 ml) hot chicken broth

8 oz. (225 g) fresh mushrooms

8 oz. (225 g) chicken livers

3 tablespoons (1 ½ oz./30 g) butter

Salt and white pepper

1 tablespoon brandy

Peel and finely chop onion. Heat oil in saucepan and sauté onion and rice until translucent. Pour in hot chicken broth and cook over gentle heat without stirring until rice is fully swelled, 20 minutes.

Wipe and trim mushrooms; cut into slices. Cut chicken livers into bite-sized pieces.

Melt half of butter in skillet and let mushrooms release their juices 10 minutes over gentle heat. Season with salt, pepper, and brandy.

Melt remaining butter in second skillet and briskly sauté livers 3 minutes, tossing. Combine with mushrooms.

Place rice on 4 serving plates and divide mushroom-liver mixture over it.

Menu Suggestion

Serve with grated Parmesan cheese and a green salad. For dessert, offer rum babas with cream.

Spaghetti with Garlic and Hot Pepper

1 lb. (450 g) spaghetti

Salt

3 garlic cloves

1 bunch parsley

5 tablespoons olive oil

1 peperoncino (small hot pepper, fresh or dried)

Grated Parmesan cheese

Cook spaghetti according to package directions in a generous amount of boiling salted water. Drain well.

While spaghetti is cooking, peel and coarsely chop garlic cloves, sprinkle with a little salt, and crush with fork (or put through garlic press without peeling). Rinse parsley, blot dry and mince.

Heat oil in small skillet and sauté garlic and hot pepper over very low heat (garlic must not brown).

Discard hot pepper after a few minutes.

In warmed bowl, thoroughly mix pasta, parsley, and garlic sauce and serve at once. Pass grated cheese separately.

> **Cooking Tip** For every 4 ounces (100 g) of pasta, boil about 3½ cups (925 ml) water with ½ teaspoon salt. To keep pasta from sticking to the bottom of the pan, stir it now, and then during cooking.

Noodles with Seafood

1 onion

2 garlic cloves

5 ripe tomatoes

3 tablespoons olive oil

1 lb. (450 g) regular or green fettuccine, or other flat noodles

Salt

8 oz. (225 g) mussels, packed in natural juices

4 oz. (100 g) shelled fresh shrimp

Black pepper

1 teaspoon dried basil

Peel onions and slice into thin rings; peel and mince garlic cloves. Blanch, peel, and chop tomatoes, coring out green stem end.

Heat 2 tablespoons oil in small saucepan and sauté onion rings and garlic until translucent. Add tomatoes and braise 10 minutes over low heat.

Cook pasta according to package directions in a generous amount of boiling salted water with remaining 1 tablespoon oil.

Drain mussels, pat shrimp dry, and add both to tomatoes. Season sauce with salt, pepper, and basil. Drain pasta, shake dry, and turn it out into warmed bowl. Serve sauce separately.

Menu Suggestion

Serve a tossed green salad. For dessert, offer warmed pecan pie with vanilla ice cream.

◁ Spaghetti with Garlic and Hot Pepper is a dish as delicious as it is economical.

Rice with Tuna

1 onion

2 tablespoons (1 oz./30 g) butter

¾ cup rice (7 oz./200 g)

2 cups (450 ml) hot beef broth

Salt and pepper

1 package (10 oz./300 g) frozen peas

2 medium tomatoes

1 can (7 oz./200 g) tuna

Peel and finely chop onion. Melt butter in saucepan and sauté onion and rice until translucent. Pour in hot broth, season rice with salt and pepper, and simmer over gentle heat until rice is fully cooked, 15 to 20 minutes, adding peas after 10 minutes.

Blanch, peel, and quarter tomatoes, coring out green stem ends. Drain tuna and flake roughly.

Carefully fold tomatoes and tuna into rice and peas; cook 5 minutes to heat through.

Fava Beans with Carrots

1 lb. (450 g) carrots

Salt

2 packages (10 oz./300 g each)
   frozen fava or lima beans

Summer savory to taste

¼ cup (60 ml) vegetable oil

1 ¾ lb. (800 g) small boiled potatoes,
   cooked the day before and peeled

6 thin slices (about 4 oz./125 g) streaky bacon

Onion powder

2 tablespoons minced fresh parsley

White pepper

Scrub carrots and cut into slices.

In large saucepan, cook carrots in a small amount of salted water for 5 minutes. Add unthawed fava beans and savory and simmer another 12 minutes.

Meanwhile, heat oil in skillet and sauté potatoes until browned.

In another skillet, fry bacon slices until crisp. Season with salt and onion powder.

Combine parsley with vegetables. Season to taste with salt, onion powder, and white pepper. Transfer vegetables to serving dish; lay bacon slices on top. Serve with sautéed potatoes.

Variation
Colorful Fava Bean Stew   Instead of carrots, use 1 to 2 packages (10 oz./300 g each) frozen mixed young summer vegetables. Cook together with fava beans. Sauté 2 peeled, chopped onions separately in 1 tablespoon vegetable oil and add to vegetables. Heat 4 flavorful smoked sausages (any preferred quick-cooking type) in the mixture. Add 2 tablespoons minced chives and serve.

Menu Suggestion
Begin with 1 smoked trout fillet per person, with grated horseradish. Accompany bean stew with a green salad and sautéed potatoes. For dessert, have vanilla-fudge ice cream and wafers.

Creamed Leeks and Shrimp

1 ¾ lb. (750 g) leeks (about 4 to 5 large leeks)

½ cup (125 ml) water

Salt

2 tablespoons (1 oz./30 g) butter

2 tablespoons all-purpose flour

1 cup (240 ml) milk

White pepper

1 tablespoon fresh lemon juice

8 oz. (225 g) shelled shrimp

3 tablespoons heavy cream

Fava Beans with Carrots: solid home fare that many people love — and love to eat again and again.   ▷

Trim and thoroughly wash leeks; cut into slices ¾ inch (2 cm) thick. Bring water to boil with salt and simmer leeks until tender, 15 minutes.

Melt butter in saucepan, sprinkle in flour and cook until light golden, stirring. A little at a time, pour in milk and bring to boil, continuing to stir. Flavor sauce with white pepper and lemon juice.

Stir in leeks (with cooking liquid) and shrimp and simmer gently 5 minutes. Stir in cream and serve.

Variation

Marseilles-Style Leeks   Prepare leeks as described above. Rinse, blanch, skin, and quarter 1 pound (450 g) tomatoes, coring out stem ends. Heat 2 tablespoons olive oil in heavy saucepan, add tomatoes and stir in cooked leeks. Stir in ½ cup (125 ml) white wine and cook briefly.

Menu Suggestion

Serve with brown rice and roasted beef or pork. For dessert, have chocolate layer cake or apple tart.

Kaiserschmarren

5 eggs

Pinch of salt

1 ⅓ cups (7 oz./200 g) all-purpose flour

1 ½ cups (380 ml) milk

¼ cup (2 oz./60 g) butter

¼ cup (60 g) sugar

Powdered sugar

Combine eggs, salt, flour, and milk in bowl and beat with whisk or electric mixer until light and foamy. Cover and let batter rest 5 minutes.

Melt half of butter in large skillet. Pour in batter all at once and cook over gentle heat until bottom is golden, shaking skillet frequently. Lift with a spatula and quickly add remaining butter to skillet. Turn pancake and cook second side.

As soon as pancake is cooked, tear into bite-size pieces with 2 forks. Sprinkle evenly with sugar and cook until golden brown.

Pile *Kaiserschmarren* onto warmed individual plates and dust with powdered sugar. Serve with applesauce, lingonberry jam, or plum compote.

Variation

Add to batter ⅓ cup (2 oz./50 g) light raisins soaked in 2 tablespoons rum. In this case you may omit the fruit compote on the side.

Apples with Calvados

4 firm medium apples

½ cup (125 ml) water

1 cup (240 ml) white wine

2 tablespoons fresh lemon juice

2 tablespoons sugar

2 tablespoons Calvados

½ cup (125 ml) seedless raspberry jam

1 pint (450 ml) vanilla ice cream

2 tablespoons sliced toasted almonds

Peel apples and cut a ''lid'' off tops. Hollow out cores to make a generous cavity in each.

Bring water and wine to boil with lemon juice and sugar. Add apples and simmer, covered, until barely tender, about 6 minutes over gentle heat.

Remove apples with slotted spoon, drain, and set in shallow bowl. While still warm, sprinkle with Calvados; allow to cool.

Warm raspberry jam in small saucepan.

Cut ice cream into small cubes and spoon some into apples; arrange remaining ice cream around the apples.

Pour hot raspberry jam over the apples, sprinkle with slivered almonds and serve at once.

Variations

You can also serve the wine-poached apples with chilled vanilla custard sauce, plain or whipped cream, or hot chocolate sauce. Rum, Cognac, or Grand Marnier can be substituted for Calvados.

◄ A filling, sweet dish — Kaiserschmarren.

Snappy Salad Ideas

To ensure variety in salads, try to keep an ample stock of canned and bottled condiments on hand — olives, pickles, pimientos, vegetables in brine, *giardiniera* relishes, and so on. Sample various bottled salad dressings to see which you prefer and then keep several kinds at the ready — an oil-and-vinegar type, a creamy mayonnaise- or buttermilk-based dressing, perhaps a cheese-flavored one.

Allow yourself a few minutes once or twice a week to wash and dry salad greens, rather than stopping to prepare them before each meal. Wrapped lightly in a towel and placed in a plastic bag, the greens can be refrigerated for days and are ready for instant use.

Try these fast homemade dressings when you'd like a change from bottled ones:

Quick Salad Dressings

Here is a basic dressing to make in quantity: Combine ¼ teaspoon salt, ¼ teaspoon white or black pepper, 1 tablespoon prepared mustard (mild or hot, depending on your taste), and 6 tablespoons red wine vinegar or herb vinegar in a jar and mix well to dissolve salt. Stir in 1 cup oil. Seal tightly and keep on the lower shelf of the refrigerator. This dressing keeps for at least 14 days. It needs only to be combined with the main salad ingredients and, if you have the time, tossed with minced fresh herbs and onion. You can also mix in a tablespoon of bottled chili sauce or soy sauce, a few dashes of hot pepper sauce, or perhaps a teaspoon of Worcestershire.

- **Mayonnaise Dressing**   Stir ¾ cup mayonnaise with 2 tablespoons evaporated milk or cream. Season with salt, a pinch of sugar, and white or black pepper. Fold in 2 tablespoons ketchup or chili sauce.
- **Fruit Dressing**   Thoroughly stir ¼ cup cream with a pinch each of salt and sugar, 3 tablespoons orange juice, and a little finely grated orange rind.
- **Yogurt Dressing**   Beat ⅔ cup yogurt until frothy; add 2 tablespoons oil. Season with salt, a pinch of sugar, and white or black pepper. Fold in 2 tablespoons ketchup or chili sauce. Enrich with 2 tablespoons cream.

Mayonnaise Dressing and Yogurt Dressing can be made the night before. The following sauces, however, must be freshly made — though they're quick enough to mix up.

- **Herb Dressing**   Whisk together ¼ cup minced fresh herbs, 2 tablespoons very finely minced onion, 2 tablespoons vinegar, a pinch each of salt, black pepper, and sugar, and 3 tablespoons oil.
- **Cream Dressing**   Beat 2 tablespoons fresh lemon juice with 6 tablespoons cream until frothy. Season with salt, a pinch of sugar, white pepper, and curry powder or mild Hungarian paprika.
- **Sour Cream Dressing**   Combine 1 tablespoon fresh lemon juice and ⅓ cup sour cream. Season with salt, a pinch of sugar, and black pepper. For more flavor you can add 2 drops hot pepper sauce or a large pinch of hot paprika. In any case, add appropriate minced herbs to the dressing.
- **Ready-Made Dressings**   There are dozens to choose from. They should be kept in the refrigerator but taken out 15 minutes before you use them to develop flavor. The thicker emulsified-type dressings can be lightened with yogurt if you wish.

Common herbs: Dill, thyme, and basil.

Mixed Salads

Here are some suggestions as to what to combine with what. Decide for yourself whether you want to add this or that extra ingredient to the vegetables I've listed, or to combine several of them. Some of these salads can serve as main dishes if tossed with substantial ingredients such as meat, fish, or cheese. The main vegetable is listed at the head of each entry. Figure on about 5 ounces (150 g) of it per person; with leafy greens 3 to 4 ounces (100 g) will be enough. Each vegetable is followed by a list of ingredients that make good combinations with it.

Snappy Salad Ideas

- **Asparagus** Mushrooms, peas and carrots, green beans, boiled ham, smoked salmon or other smoked fish.
- **Beans, Green** Onions, bell peppers, tomatoes, julienne of ham or sausage.
- **Beets** Can be served as is from the jar or used in a salad of onions, apples, pears, boiled potatoes, roast veal, chopped walnuts, hard-cooked eggs, matjes herring fillets.
- **Bell Peppers, Canned Mild Cherry Peppers, Pimientos or Roasted Red Peppers** Tomatoes, escarole, endive, apples, olives, anchovies.
- **Chinese Cabbage** Tangerine segments, hard-cooked eggs, tomatoes, chopped walnuts, bell peppers, anchovy fillets, tuna, roast meat; use soy-sauce dressing.

- **Celery Root** Apples, pineapples, onions, sweet pickles, grapes, chopped walnuts; serve with cream-based dressing.
- **Corn** Bell peppers, peas, onions, broiled poultry.
- **Cucumbers** Lettuce, tomatoes, onions, radishes, plenty of dill.
- **Endive** Tangerine or orange segments, tomatoes, onions, chopped walnuts, radishes, hard cheeses such as pecorino.
- **Escarole** Tangerine segments or cut-up peaches, tomatoes or bell peppers.
- **Fennel** Orange segments, apples, pears, anchovies.
- **Lettuce** Tomatoes, cucumbers, bell peppers, apples, tangerine segments, chopped walnuts or hazelnuts.
- **Mushrooms** Hard-cooked eggs, cut-up asparagus, poultry, roast meat.
- **Peas** Onions, corn, asparagus, sausage, pecorino cheese.
- **Peas and Carrots** Wild or cultivated mushrooms, hard-cooked eggs, sausage, cheese.
- **Radishes** Lettuce, tomatoes, cucumbers, tuna, matjes herring.
- **Sauerkraut** Apples, pears, pineapple, orange or tangerine segments, cooked smoked pork loin, mild salami.
- **Tomatoes** Cucumbers, leaf lettuce, onions, pears, corn, peas, beans, sweet pickles, bell peppers or canned mild cherry peppers or pimientos, roast meat or smoked fish.

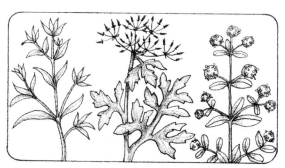

Less familiar herbs: Tarragon, chervil, and marjoram

Tips for Quick Desserts

The market is brimming with tempting desserts, ready to serve in cartons, cups, or goblets or prepared to the point that only one or two ingredients need to be added. You'll find instant custard and pudding mixes, flans and whips, even chocolate mousse. There are layered desserts of fruit and yogurt and a myriad of frozen concoctions. And don't neglect the deli counter's ready-made rice or bread puddings.

Instant dessert mixes must be mixed with milk, water, or cream, often with some additional ingredient. Desserts prepared with fresh milk are especially nourishing for children. The mixing usually takes 1 minute; the dish must then rest another 15 to 20 minutes until set. These desserts should be mixed before you begin making the rest of the meal, so they'll be ready when it's time for dessert. You can also make them the evening before, pour the mixture into individual serving dishes and keep them in the refrigerator covered with clear plastic wrap. Most will not change consistency by the next day. All these desserts are ideal for cooking on the go. And because they take so little time, they often leave you a few extra minutes to arrange a pretty garnish or presentation. Some suggestions follow.

Fast and Festive Garnishes

- **Whipped Cream** With this you can saddle any dessert with a few more calories! Actually, there's hardly a dessert that cream doesn't go well with.
- **Fruit** Tangerine segments, peach slices, pineapple chunks, cherries, yellow plums, blueberries and other berries, fresh, canned or packed in jars, do well with vanilla- or almond-flavored desserts as well as those based on chocolate, yogurt, or cottage cheese.
- **Nuts** Whether it's almonds, pistachios, walnuts, or hazelnuts–chopped, sliced, or slivered–they give extra pizzazz to a lot of ready-made desserts and to instant puddings.
- **Cookies and Small Pastries** Crown each dessert serving with a macaroon, little meringue kisses, or small sweet biscuits.
- **Chocolate** Coarsely grated or shaved chocolate, very lightly dusted with powdered sugar, adds a touch of elegance. Or use chocolate wafers, nonpareils, "bark" chocolate, miniature pralines, or chocolate "coffee beans."
- **Candied Fruit** Many people love these supersweet fruits, which are sold whole and in chunks. They lend color and eye appeal to pud-

dings, custards, and other desserts. To this category also belong chopped candied lemon and orange rind and finely diced ginger in syrup. Because of their intense flavor, use these last ingredients sparingly.

- **Spirits** Finally, any dessert can be dressed up with, for example, rum, Cointreau, fruit liqueurs, and egg-based liqueurs like *Advocaat* and Mexican *Rompope*. Pour alternate layers of an egg-based or Irish cream-type drink and instant pudding or custard into parfait glasses, and serve with a garnish for a flavorful and attractive dessert. Beyond this, discover for yourself what suits what. You might garnish a chocolate dessert with additional grated chocolate, a vanilla dessert with fruit. There are no limits to your fancy. And there's no quarreling over taste,' either. After all, no one is going to stop you from creating fanciful garnishes, or from cheerfully substituting chocolate for fruit or sweet biscuits and whipped cream for nuts.

A final tip for a really luscious treat: in a dessert glass, alternate layers of mocha, caramel, or chocolate custard or pudding with coconut flakes lightly steeped in orange liqueur.

Other Sweet Touches

- **Fruit Compotes** Canned or packed in jars or put up at home; also, pureed fruits like apples or apple-raspberry sauce.
- **Plain Unwhipped Cream** This is ideal for fruit puddings, but also tastes very good with chocolate, caramel, and nut desserts. And with plain cream you save the time you'd need to whip it.
- **Chocolate Sauce or Syrup** Admirably suited to vanilla and fruit desserts, also to *crème caramel*, flan and many other purchased preparations.
- **Fruit Sauces** These come in bottles, in orange, raspberry, blueberry, apricot, and other flavors. They are elegant with (for example) wine custards, or fruit puddings.
- **No-cook Custard Sauces** Also on the market, available in both vanilla and chocolate.

I haven't forgotten the vast palette of ice creams and frozen desserts. But I'd like to add here that an ice cream luscious to begin with can be made even better by means of choice sauces — hot chocolate sauce, for instance — and a quickie garnish or fruit.

Conversion Table

Note that the recipes in this book feature both U.S. customary and metric measurements. For cooks in Great Britain, Canada, and Australia, note the following information for imperial measurements. If you are familiar with metric measurements, then we recommend you follow those, incorporated into every recipe. If not, then use these conversions to achieve best results. Bear in mind that ingredients such as flour vary greatly and you will have to make some adjustments.

Liquid Measures

The British cup is larger than the American. The Australian cup is smaller than the British but a little larger than the American. Use the following cup measurements for liquids, making the adjustments as indicated.

U.S.	1 cup (236 ml)
British and Canadian	1 cup (284 ml)–adjust measurement to ¼ pint + 2 tablespoons
Australian	1 cup (250 ml)–adjust measurement to ¼ pint

Weight and Volume Measures

U.S. cooking procedures usually measure certain items by volume, although in other countries these items are often measured by weight. Here are some approximate equivalents for basic items.

	U.S. Customary	Metric	Imperial
Butter	1 cup	250 g	8 ounces
	½ cup	125 g	4 ounces
	¼ cup	62 g	2 ounces
	1 tablespoon	15 g	½ ounce
Flour (sifted all-purpose or plain)	1 cup	128 g	4¼ ounces
	½ cup	60 g	2⅛ ounces
	¼ cup	32 g	1 ounce
Sugar (caster)	1 cup	240 g	8 ounces
	½ cup	120 g	4 ounces
	1 tablespoon	15 g	½ ounce
Chopped vegetables	1 cup	115 g	4 ounces
	½ cup	60 g	2 ounces
Chopped meats or fish	1 cup	225 g	8 ounces
	½ cup	110 g	4 ounces

Index

Index